# APOSTOLIC EVOLUTION

*Your Transition Between Apostolic Cycles*

## COLETTE TOACH

BEST SELLING AUTHOR

ColetteToachStore.com

# Apostolic Evolution

Author: Colette Toach
Graphics & Cover Design: Jessica Toach

**ISBN-13:** 978-1-62664-272-0
eBook ISBN: 978-1-62664-271-3
Kindle ISBN: 978-1-62664-273-7
iBooks ISBN: 978-1-62664-274-4

Copyright © 2026 by Apostolic Movement International, LLC.
All rights reserved
5663 Balboa Ave #416,
San Diego,
California 92111,
United States of America

**1st Printing January 2026**

Published by **Apostolic Movement International, LLC**
E-mail Address: admin@ami-bookshop.com
Web Address: www.ami-bookshop.com

All rights reserved under International Copyright Law.
Contents may not be reproduced in whole or in part in any form without the express written consent of the publisher.

Unless specified, all Scripture references taken from the New King James Version®. Copyright © 1982 by Thomas Nelson. Used by permission. All rights reserved.

# Table of Contents

**Prologue Apostolic Evolution** ................................................................. - 9 -

*Joshua Would You Please Step Up!* ........................................................ - 10 -
    What Failure Looks Like.................................................................... - 12 -

*No, You Are Not Being Unfaithful!* ......................................................... - 13 -

*Caleb – You Got This!* ............................................................................ - 14 -
    The Season for Action Is Now............................................................ - 16 -

**1 An Apostolic Message** ........................................................................ - 19 -

*The Authority of the Office* ................................................................... - 19 -

*The Land You Fought For* ...................................................................... - 21 -
    And Then It Was 2020....................................................................... - 23 -

*From Warrior to Kingdom Builder* ......................................................... - 24 -

**2 Diversity of Church Types** ................................................................... - 27 -

*Rejoicing in Our Diversity* ...................................................................... - 28 -

*New Church Types* ................................................................................ - 29 -
    The Movie Church ............................................................................ - 30 -
    Finding Balance................................................................................ - 32 -

*International Positioning* ...................................................................... - 33 -

**3 The Sleeper Apostles** ......................................................................... - 35 -

*Joseph*................................................................................................... - 35 -
    The Price: You're Not Allowed "Normal" ........................................... - 36 -

*Esther and Mordecai* ............................................................................. - 37 -
    You Are Not Alone............................................................................ - 38 -

*Diversity of Mandates* ................................................................ *- 39 -*
   Dial Down the Judgment ........................................................ - 39 -
   Smashing Limitations on Your Mandate ............................... - 40 -

*Anointing Required* .................................................................... *- 40 -*

## 4 Your Process to Discovering the "More" ................................ - 43 -

*Embrace the Transition* ............................................................. *- 44 -*
   Did I Just Lose My Anointing? .............................................. - 45 -

*Shift a Little!* ............................................................................... *- 45 -*

*The Solomon Model* ................................................................... *- 46 -*
   Do More Than "Go Into Ministry" ........................................ - 48 -

*Revolutionize Your Perspective* ................................................ *- 50 -*

## 5 Apostolic Types in the Movement ........................................ - 53 -

*David – The Tradition Breaker* .................................................. *- 53 -*

*Joseph – The Undercover Businessman* .................................... *- 54 -*

*Esther and Mordecai – Political Kingdom Changers* ............... *- 55 -*

*Nehemiah – Leaders of the Prophetic Movement* .................... *- 56 -*

*Ezra – Church and Ministry Planters* ....................................... *- 57 -*

*What Land Is Yours?* .................................................................. *- 59 -*
   Making the Relationship Transition ..................................... - 60 -

*Watching Your Promises Burn* .................................................. *- 60 -*
   Adjusting from the Wilderness Mentality to Prosperity ..... - 62 -

## 6 You Are the Church .............................................................. - 65 -

*Why Has Revival Tarried?* ......................................................... *- 66 -*

*The Journey* ................................................................................ *- 67 -*
   Complete Segregation ............................................................ - 68 -
   The Spirit of the World .......................................................... - 69 -

*The Church of the Future* .......................................................... *- 70 -*
   A Church Without Walls ....................................................... - 70 -

**7 A Trendsetting Church** .................................................................. - 73 -

    *YOU Are the City on a Hill* ........................................................ - 74 -

    *A Church of Influence and Power* ............................................ - 75 -

    *Breaking Ministry Mindsets* ..................................................... - 76 -

    *The King's Advisors* .................................................................. - 77 -

    *Become a Tare* .......................................................................... - 79 -

    *The Pajama Apostle* ................................................................. - 81 -

**8 Identify the Season of Mandate Completion** ....................... - 83 -

    *A Fragmented Vision* ............................................................... - 84 -

    *How Mandates Come to an End* ............................................. - 85 -

    *1. Mandate Is Completed – Establishing a Monument* .......... - 85 -

    *2. Mandate Cannot Be Completed* ........................................... - 87 -

    *3. You Pass the Mandate On* .................................................... - 89 -

    *The Transition Between Mandates – Your Damascus Road Experience* - 91 -
        Emptied for Purpose ........................................................... - 93 -

    *New Perspective on the Horizon* .............................................. - 94 -

    *The Apostolic Movement Is Upon Us* ...................................... - 96 -

**9 From Tabernacle to Temple** ..................................................... - 99 -

    *Tent of Meeting* ....................................................................... - 100 -
        The Rain Is Coming ............................................................ - 101 -

    *Apostolic Evolution* ................................................................. - 102 -
        What Will You Pass On? .................................................... - 103 -

    *Dare You Step Out and Fly?* ................................................... - 106 -

    *The Tabernacle of David* ........................................................ - 107 -

    *Season to Season* .................................................................... - 109 -

**10 Making the Temple Transition** ............................................ - 111 -

1. What Is the One Thing You Do Not Want to Give Up?.................- 111 -
2. What Feels Like It has Died? .......................................................- 112 -

*Apostolic Trendsetters* ......................................................................- 113 -
Changing the Tide ........................................................................- 115 -

*A New Pattern*....................................................................................- 115 -
Abraham... Let's Take a Hike!......................................................- 116 -

*Burn the Promises* .............................................................................- 117 -
Make the Transition Already! .....................................................- 118 -

## 11 The Three Realms that Denote Apostolic Maturity ........................- 121 -

*The Three Realms* ..............................................................................- 123 -
Welcome to a New Era ................................................................- 124 -

*Some Church Realities That Need to Change*....................................- 125 -
What's Wrong With People? .......................................................- 126 -

*Your Apostolic Blueprint* ...................................................................- 126 -
Get Your House in Order, Apostle................................................- 127 -
The Anointing Empowers You......................................................- 128 -

*Establishing Apostolic Structure* .......................................................- 129 -
Show Me Your Pattern in Writing................................................- 129 -

*The Early Church Pattern* ..................................................................- 130 -

## 12 The Ministry Realm: Your Temple.................................................- 133 -

Requirements to Build .................................................................- 134 -

*Transition From War to Peace is a Battle!*.........................................- 134 -
Smoke Those Snakes Out!...........................................................- 135 -
Mindset Shift Required ................................................................- 137 -
Fivefold Ministry Positioning .......................................................- 137 -
The Fruit That Remains ...............................................................- 138 -
Respecting the Pages of Your Story ............................................- 139 -

*Gathering God's Generals*..................................................................- 139 -

*DNA Exchange* ...................................................................................- 140 -
Adding the Missing Pieces ...........................................................- 141 -

*Finding Connection* ............................................................ - 142 -

*Establishing a Kingdom* ..................................................... - 143 -
   Extending Your Reach ................................................... - 143 -

*An Apostolic Network* ........................................................ - 144 -

*Your Spiritual DNA Will Come Through* ............................. - 145 -

## 13 The Business Realm: Your Ships of Tarshish ............ - 147 -

*Develop Your Business Pattern* ......................................... - 150 -

*Changing Business Mindsets* ............................................ - 151 -
   You Are Not of This World! .............................................. - 151 -
   Who Really Made You Rich? ............................................ - 152 -

*The Holy Spirit Difference* ................................................ - 153 -

*How You Develop That Power* .......................................... - 154 -

*1. Study to Show Yourself Approved* ................................. - 155 -
   Embrace the Business Realm Process ........................... - 157 -

*2. Positioning Through Obedience* .................................... - 158 -

*3. Send Out Your Ships* ..................................................... - 160 -
   Taking Steps Forward ..................................................... - 161 -

*Each Realm Follows a Clear Pattern* ................................. - 162 -

*Is Your Temple Going to Remain?* ..................................... - 163 -
   Switching up Our Money Mentality ................................ - 163 -

*What Does Your Business Realm Look Like?* .................... - 164 -

## 14 The Social Realm: Building Your Palace ................... - 167 -

*Relationships Are Key* ....................................................... - 168 -

*1. Evolution of Your Identity* ............................................. - 169 -
   Wake up to the Signs! ..................................................... - 171 -

*2. Gain Favor by Keeping Up!* ............................................ - 172 -
   Social Media .................................................................... - 174 -

*3. Make Friends* ................................................................. - 174 -

*You Are the Pattern* .................................................................................. *- 178 -*

*Take Action* ............................................................................................... *- 179 -*

**About the Author** .......................................................................................... **181**

*Let's Build a Relationship* ........................................................................ *182*

**Recommendations by the Author** ............................................................ **- 185 -**

*The Apostolic Handbook* ..................................................................... *- 185 -*

*Apostolic Mandate* ................................................................................ *- 186 -*

# Prologue

## Apostolic Evolution

**Evolution:** *The gradual process of change and development in something, often leading to greater complexity, adaptation, or advancement (Combination of Oxford English Dictionary (OED) and Merriam-Webster)*

The apostolic journey is a series of seasons. Each one borrowing elements from the first and adding complexity to the next. Nothing discourages an apostle more than looking at a past season and feeling underwhelmed by it. You want to see fruit in summer from the seeds you sowed in winter.

Sometimes you don't correctly identify your seasons. And this is where our journey begins. Your season has changed and as you stand in transition, I'm here to help you make the next leap in your evolution. Together we will dig deeper into the realm of the Spirit. We will delve into the complexity of your mandate. Then finally we will set clear structures in place for advancement.

God put this book in your hand for this Kairos time. Receive the impartation and seasons past will make sense.

The Father is calling on us to usher in a move of His making and He is calling us to take our place.

In many ways, our training never ends. Like Moses, we grow with each challenge we overcome. However, we cannot be in perpetual training. There needs to come a time when we become discontent with our environment enough to do something about it.

The gifts, authority, and anointing you've received from the Father were never for your benefit. They were elements of grace imparted to you from heaven to bring actionable change in the earth. Whether your grace is to be added in the arts, business, community, or local church, is up to where God positioned you.

## Joshua Would You Please Step Up!

A new generation cries out for us to lead them. Moses has climbed to the mountain top and he has surveyed the land. He has rested heavily on his staff, weary of the journey. With one last glimpse of what is to be, the Lord has spirited him away.

Now it's time for Joshua to pick up where Moses left off and to lead a generation that sees the world with very new eyes. They're a bold and courageous generation who are ready to do whatever it takes to build. They will foolishly walk around the walls of Jericho until they fall. They will boldly declare the Word of God and be unashamed of who their Father is.

The question is, "Are you gutsy enough to lead such a new generation?" Do you have the courage to evolve and lead a generation that stands armed and ready for war? To lead such a generation means becoming the kind of leader that they want to pattern themselves after.

I came from a family of pastors on both sides of my parents. I grew up with stories of what God did in the past. Yet, I look back and although I admire the price that they paid for me to stand where I do today, I also realize that I cannot do things the same way.

My message is preached with new flavor. Our revelation of the prophetic and apostolic in this Church era has bust open the limited view of our patriarchs.

They saw through a mirror dimly and today we embrace the fullness of our responsibility to build the Kingdom. We stand where we do because of the great men and women who have gone before us: Spiritual mothers and fathers who imparted to us, great leaders who inspired us to greatness.

Thing is though, it's time to evolve. The way they did things worked for their generation! The land before us looks nothing like they had to face and while doctrinal principles remain the same through the years, the implementation of that doctrine changes generation after generation.

So yes, can the Joshuas and Solomons please step up?! Daddy did a great job, but now it's time for you to take the lead and to complete what he began. Solomon didn't overcome with the tip of the sword, but rather with the wisdom of wealth. Joshua was a man of war who had the authority to tell the sun to stand still.

They both followed in their fathers' footsteps but expressed themselves for the generations that they led.

## What Failure Looks Like

Do you want to see what it looks like when you refuse to evolve?

> ***2 Chronicles 10:16*** *Now when all Israel saw that the king didn't listen to them, the people answered the king, saying:*
> *"What share have we in David?*
> *We have no inheritance in the son of Jesse.*
> *Every man to your tents, O Israel!*
> *Now see to your own house, O David!"*
> *So, all of Israel departed to their tents.*

Rehoboam and his buddies really didn't get the memo. Even the elders of his time could see that times had changed. They had the common sense to listen to the word on the ground. The people had changed. Times had changed.

Unfortunately, Rehoboam was too busy living it up coasting on what his father accomplished and didn't realize that to rule well, he needed to evolve. He needed to take what his father had passed on to him and make it his own with the people he now led.

Unfortunately, he lost most of the kingdom, with only Judah sticking to him. The Lord brought His word to pass by causing Rehoboam to stay stuck in his ways. If you refuse to evolve you'll limit God's capacity to use you. This means allowing Him to displace the way you think and the way you've done ministry until this point.

# No, You Are Not Being Unfaithful!

I feel that this needs to be said. Allowing the Lord to evolve how you operate is not a sign that you're unfaithful to your previous spiritual father. When we are like Solomon, Aaron, Timothy and Joshua, we cling to what our spiritual fathers invested into us. Indeed, they deserve the honor and respect for the price that they paid to do the work of God.

However, obligation should never hinder you from evolving in your apostolic walk. When my parents were teenagers, fashion didn't allow for comfy sneakers and stretch denim! Should I've continued to wear my mother's clothing as an adult? Does this mean I don't respect my mother? Just because I don't want to wear her clothes, does this mean I'm rejecting her? Hardly! In the same way, when the Lord begins to evolve you in your call, you're not being unfaithful to the memory and hard work of your previous spiritual father.

Rather, you're taking the seed that they invested into you and you're planting it! You only know the true color of a blossom once the seed has sprouted and the plant bloomed. It's indeed the cycle of life. They imparted a seed, but you're called to reap a harvest. It's a different process and it's time that you let go of the obligation and shake loose of the straight jacket that you find yourself bound up in!

Do not fool yourself! You have been conditioned for many years to think and minister the way that you do. So, breaking free is not as simple as making a decision. It's going to take processing and perhaps if you realize that, you'll also recognize the pressures all around you at the moment.

The Lord blessed Craig and I with a young team. There came a time when I hit the wall in the "building my palace" part of my process. I stepped back and realized that my perspective was limited. I allowed them to challenge me to see the world through their eyes. It began a process in me that continues to evolve me and so it evolves my temple, trading ships, and palace!

If you ever find yourself touting your many years in ministry and your age as a reason to impart your wisdom, then you're not ready for this new move. I've met a lot of unwise old people! One of those being someone who said to me once, "I don't need to take this course or study, because I've been in ministry for 22 years." In that moment they expressed their ignorance very loudly!

Anyone who has truly grown for the full 22 years of ministry recognizes that the more you grow, the more you need to grow. The more you learn, the more ignorant you feel. The more perspective you receive, the more you realize you need to see.

The more I hear the voice of my Savior, the more I crave His presence, and the more I want to know about Him. I go to bed at night thinking to myself, "There is still so much to learn and accomplish!" May I never outgrow this mindset. May I never get so old that I think my number of years is a substitute for wisdom and revelation.

## CALEB – YOU GOT THIS!

> ***Joshua 14:11*** *As yet I'm as strong this day as on the day that Moses sent me; just as my strength was then, so now is my strength for war, both for going out and for*

*coming in.*
*12 Now therefore, give me this mountain of which the LORD spoke in that day; for you heard in that day how the Anakim were there, and that the cities were great and fortified. It may be that the LORD will be with me, and I shall be able to drive them out as the LORD said."*

Caleb was 85 when he made this statement. Does this sound like someone who is stuck in the past? Hardly! He was ready to strap a sword to his side and take the enemy on. No way he was going to let his promised land go! That we would all have the fire that Caleb did! Not only did he stand against all the spies when scoping out the Promised Land the first time round, but when his turn came, he took his land with both hands!

He evolved along with the new generation that was born. Age has nothing to do with it. Are you prepared to evolve? Caleb didn't consider himself too old to take hold of his promises. Neither should we become too old to take the land God has promised for His Church!

This means allowing Him to pick us up and lead us into war, time and again. So yes, perhaps you've outlived a number of spiritual leaders. Perhaps you've had a number of spiritual fathers whose footsteps you've followed in. Well, you can continue to look back or you could walk forward now.

Take the seeds each planted and sow them so that the Church can eat of its fruit. Lay to rest the guilt you may be carrying from the seasons that have passed. I'm going to say it again, Apostle, you cannot walk forward looking back. You are not being unfaithful to Moses. You are not sinning. You are evolving and you're pleasing your heavenly Father who has ordered your steps.

Do not allow the memory of the greats to fall into the dust by not paying the price forward. We allow too much bondage to restrict us from fulfilling God's plan. Once again, remember that this call is not for you! This is not about fulfilling your purpose. This is about fulfilling God's purpose. This is not about your call, but about God's plan.

You now have your spiritual family to raise and a new spiritual DNA to impart. Your DNA strand, along with mine and the apostles all over the world stand ready to move forward.

## THE SEASON FOR ACTION IS NOW

Like I already said, now is not the time to run around and find tools and armor. Like Caleb, you should already know how to fight. So, what if you missed your season? What if you didn't fulfill the part that God required of you when you had the time?

Well, sitting and regretting it, will not change a thing! You can only stand in confidence, realizing that the entire world will not come to a grinding halt because you failed to fulfill your part in perfect time. Rather, you can pick up what you do have and start to build.

You can establish the land you've. You can lead the generation that's following you. You can walk through the open doors at your face. There is no time to mourn those who fell in the wilderness and while their memories will always remain with us, we cannot raise them from their slumber. Our regrets, fears, and great losses are now monuments to the past. They will always be a reminder of where we have come from. They will serve as a picture of what inspired us as a Church.

However, Apostle, a movement has begun. You stand on the threshold of a realization that many desired to see but never did. The Father has positioned and trained you. So, come now, take my hand and let us build!

# 1

# An Apostolic Message

I am calling those out who have an apostolic calling on their lives and called of God to change, establish, and set a new pattern for the Church.

> *I'M CALLING THOSE OUT WHO HAVE AN APOSTOLIC CALLING ON THEIR LIVES AND HAVE BEEN CALLED OF GOD TO CHANGE, ESTABLISH, AND SET A NEW PATTERN FOR THE CHURCH.*

I'm calling the leaders out who were born with eyes to see and ears to hear. I'm calling those who have received a call directly from the Father. So, please don't think that reading this book will give you your call.

Rather, I'm calling out those who already received the call from the Father and are standing with a sword in one hand and a shield in the other, saying, "God, where to from here?"

## The Authority of the Office

Now that I've set the tone, realize that we have quite a landscape to explore together here. The apostolic movement is upon us whether we like it or not. As an apostle, you've been thrown around, shifted, and sifted. Now that all has been said and done, I'm here to peel back the layers and make sense of your process.

In addition to that, I will help you document the artifacts that you've uncovered along the way. It's time to recognize your place in the apostolic move. In fact, Apostle, it's time to step into the office.

It's one thing to flow in a gift or two, it's another to function in apostolic office.

The real power comes, when you walk in the authority of the office. This means embracing your diversity so that you can recognize the diversity of this movement.

*THE REAL POWER COMES WHEN YOU WALK IN THE AUTHORITY OF THE OFFICE.*

It might mean acting as Apostle Paul who stepped into the unknown with a message no one else dared to utter! Even Apostle Peter who opened the door to the Gentiles couldn't fathom Paul's message. How often has your voice been silenced? How many more times will you build a work, only to have others come and preach a different gospel?

There is this hope though, Apostle. What the Lord has begun, He will also finish. The perfection of our patriarchs didn't determine the continuation of the Early Church. Rather it depended on the power of the Spirit. Our part? To walk in boldness. This often means having the courage to stand alone.

It means having the humility to go back to the drawing board time and again. It also means recognizing that your journey was never to establish your platform. Rather, it was a long thread designed to be woven in the fabric of an apostolic movement.

# The Land You Fought For

You feel it, don't you? The shifting sands beneath your feet. Relationships, ministries and gifts are all in flux.

You have "done ministry" but no matter how much the Lord has used you, you recognize that you've yet to embrace the fullness of who you're called to be.

*YOU HAVE "DONE MINISTRY" BUT NO MATTER HOW MUCH THE LORD HAS USED YOU, YOU RECOGNIZE THAT YOU'VE YET TO EMBRACE THE FULLNESS OF WHO YOU'RE CALLED TO BE.*

So, stop for a minute, Apostle, and survey the land around you. The Lord has gone to great lengths to position you where you stand today. If you'll be silent for a moment, you'll feel a shaking beneath your feet. For many years you've pursued your promised land. For years, you've fought, prayed, and invested in God's people.

Today you stand in a position for the Lord to sweep you up in the apostolic movement that He had begun years ago. What was but a rumbling under the earth is now becoming a shaking that the Church feels universally. In fact, you and apostles all over the world are positioned in lands, people, and circumstances they didn't begin with.

Just like Abraham, you were called to leave the familiar. If you stop and look around, you'd discover that you're overlooking the land you fought for.

It may be a land that you love, or it may be a land that you hate. It might be a huge land, or it might be a small land. Regardless,

I'm here to tell you that you've taken your land. You've spent years doing that!

There came a time when the children of Israel came to the end of their wars. They had years of it. There was war after war, blood spilled for generations. This is certainly how it feels as we look at the history of the Church. Perhaps it's how you feel as you look at your own land. You fought hard... war after war. One blood battle after another. Listen up though, Apostle!

The seasons have changed and it's time to become solidified in your place in this apostolic move.

> ***Ecclesiastes 3:2*** *A time to be born,*
> *And a time to die;*
> *A time to plant,*
> *And a time to pluck what is planted;*
>
> ***Ecclesiastes 3:8*** *A time to love,*
> *And a time to hate;*
> *A time of war,*
> *And a time of peace.*

We get so caught up fighting for land all the time that it's pretty hard to imagine that we have "arrived." Truthfully, there is always a new level to go to as an apostle. However, there are seasons when we have to sink our roots deep and work the land we have!

We can be so busy pressing forward for the greater and latter rain that we don't realize how much we already have. Yes, you had your season of warfare. Yes, you had to push through. However, if you look around, you would see that you indeed have land in your hands today.

*THE SEASONS HAVE CHANGED AND IT'S TIME TO BECOME SOLIDIFIED IN YOUR PLACE IN THIS APOSTOLIC MOVE.*

## AND THEN IT WAS 2020...

You have an opportunity, an open door, and possibilities right in front of you. What did you think all those dramatic shifts in your circumstances were all about? Did you think that the Lord rearranged your ministry in all these years just for the fun of it? No, He made a promise. You obeyed. Circumstances plucked you up and then planted you smack-bang in the middle of a land you've fought very hard for.

Perhaps it doesn't look like much at the moment. It might not even be the land you anticipated. I can say this though, in my walk with the Lord as an apostle, when He brought His promises to pass, they never came to pass as I anticipated.

He told me in 2019 that He was preparing us for expansion for 2020. He pressed often saying, "Time is running out." I thought, "Ah ha! This means that the Lord wants us to go on a ministry tour of the United States. That must be the expansion He was talking about."

Umm... not so much. 2020 struck and a worldwide pandemic closed borders, banned travel, and locked everyone away with all the toilet paper they could scrounge and an entirely new family dynamic to figure out.

All of a sudden 2019 made sense. In 2019 we established efficient online systems and 2020 facilitated the unprecedented growth we saw our ministry experience. Did I recognize my land while up to my neck in bloody battlefields?

Hardly. It took a shift in circumstances and a day-to-day obedience to recognize that God's picture of what this promised land would look like was nothing like my own.

## From Warrior to Kingdom Builder

Let me tell you, Apostle, there's only one time when the land will truly be yours. It's not when you win it. Instead, ownership is solidified when you build on it. It's when you establish the land that God has given you.

*WE'RE SO USED TO FIGHTING FOR OUR LAND THAT WE GET CAUGHT UP IN A WARRIOR MENTALITY.*

The problem is that we're so used to fighting for our land that we get caught up in a warrior mentality. We've been fighting for so long, that it will take a bit of a shift in the way that we think.

The Lord tried to warn me time and again. He said to me, "Colette, the sand is about to shift under your feet because I need you to change the way that you think. Until now, you've always fought for the next level. You push hard, strive, and reach forward. However, you don't stop long enough to see the land that you've won."

There came a time when the children of Israel needed to take a time of rest. Time to establish their families, build their homes, and establish cities. They only became a kingdom after that.

We're known as the Kingdom of God, but when I look in the spirit, am I seeing a well-built Kingdom, or one always at war?

Don't get me wrong, there will always be warfare and more land that we need to fight for.

However, if we don't take time, in the now, to establish what we do have, where is the base from which we can fight from tomorrow?

> HOWEVER, IF WE DON'T TAKE TIME, IN THE NOW, TO ESTABLISH WHAT WE DO HAVE, WHERE IS THE BASE FROM WHICH WE CAN FIGHT FROM TOMORROW?

If your focus is on continually breaking new ground, how will you see an established kingdom that others can live in?

So let's have a look at how far the Church has come, and let's realize that God is about to bring a move that's designed to establish us as a kingdom.

# 2

# DIVERSITY OF CHURCH TYPES

Apostle, you've been at war for a very long time. You're weary. You've withstood opposition. Here is an encouraging word for you: Every great move has had opposition. If you didn't have opposition, then you're not through your process yet.

Nobody likes change. Of course, you'll face opposition. You are rocking the boat. Look at the Twelve (thirteen with Paul).

They were crucified, beheaded, and beaten. Of course, there is going to be opposition! Yet, I'm here to tell you that not only is there a reason for it, but it's time for you to pick up the sword that opposition lent to you and to use it to fulfill your purpose.

It's time for you to wake up out of this slumber and use those spiritual muscles God has given you. The opposition you survived has imparted the power to overcome. You didn't allow the opposition to crush you. You didn't allow it to waylay you from the vision. Rather, each time you got up again, you stood strengthened. And so, now the Church is ready, and it needs you and the strength you've gained through the process.

*THE OPPOSITION YOU SURVIVED HAS IMPARTED THE POWER TO OVERCOME.*

## Rejoicing in Our Diversity

Our generation has seen the rise of the megachurch.

They boast tens and hundreds of thousands of congregation members. Many become members after they get saved.

They're the pretty churches that are outfitted with smoke machines, lights, and gather the crowds. Their mission is usually quite evangelistic. Meetings are a big party, and they have community groups for everything.

I'm not knocking it. I'm saying that it exists, and it has a purpose in the Church. However, this is not all there is to church.

There are also those who grew up in this environment with a fire for God and a call on their lives. After maturing, they looked at "church" and said, "If I want some depth and meat, I will have to go somewhere else."

And so, we've seen a shift in the last fifteen years. We've begun to see the rise of prophetic and apostolic churches.

So, we have prophetic and apostolic churches scattered throughout the Church universal. I preached against such churches for the longest time. I thought, "Why call yourself a prophetic church? We're all just a church, right?"

The Lord said to me, "That is just the beginning. I'm diversifying. Do not knock it! You are a member of my body, and there are many members in my body. Not every member will look alike. Every church will serve its purpose."

Since then we've seen the rise of apostolic and prophetic hubs in every nation. Places of equipping. Usually accompanied by an emphasis on going out to duplicate and equip.

## DIVERSITY OF CHURCH TYPES

Each of us has a picture of what church should be, right? We have our ideas of what the service should look like, what the preacher should preach.

However, we need to recognize that God is bringing diversity to His Church. Prophetic and apostolic churches are just the tip of the iceberg.

# New Church Types

In this season, we'll see business ministries and churches of many types founded. There'll be arts churches. Churches whose mandate revolves around making movies, writing music, and putting on massive productions.

> *IN THIS SEASON, WE'LL SEE BUSINESS MINISTRIES AND CHURCHES OF MANY TYPES FOUNDED.*

"What?! Now, we are really going into the devil's camp. Are you kidding me? We're going to have churches that are making movies?"

I heard stories from the old days. I'm blessed. I come from a couple of generations of Christians. So, I heard a lot of first-hand accounts of the movements through the years, not from books, but from my family.

I my grandparents sharing how Christians started to use radio to preach the gospel. Traditionalists threw a fit! "Oh, my goodness! That's the devil. The Church is using radio to preach the Word?"

I sit here wondering how they would feel seeing churches all over the world streaming meetings over social media and Zoom!

Imagine for a moment how horrified our great-grandparents would be to see us having praise and worship outdoors and smashing every known concept of "orderly church agenda."

You hear that now and you want to laugh. You think, "Come on guys... catch up!"

Not so fast because I'm saying the same thing to you today. It's time for you to catch up!

God is about to use His Church in a much broader capacity than before. We're a body, and we are His bride. We're meant to be influencing this world. I'm so excited to look in the Church and see the likes of Pure Flix and leaders like the Kendrick brothers, releasing movies that people, both saved and unsaved, are lining up to watch.

Unbelievers are paying to watch our message at movie houses and streaming them on their tablets.

Do you feel called to the arts and feel drawn to start a church like that? Your first push back will come from those with pre-conceived ideas of what church should look like.

Then, in your own mind, because you've never seen it any other way, you feel that you're doing something wrong. I want you to know that you're exactly where God needs you to be.

## The Movie Church

I had an opportunity to minister to somebody whom God called from within the entertainment industry. He became powerfully born again, and today he has a movie church. Everyone in his church are movie stars, actors, and struggling actors. He mentors and trains them. They have church together, and they understand one another.

They work in an industry that no other Christian understands. Am I going to walk into such a meeting and tell them how they should have church?

I know my limitation. Sure, I can maybe preach a principle or two. Sure, I can bring them the gospel. However, would I really have what they need for where they're at, with my lifestyle and where I come from?

How could I give them tools to reach others for Christ in the environment that they're in?

That takes grit. It takes a mandate, a call. We'll see more and more of these churches that seem to clump around a specific agenda.

I've seen this even in local churches. For you pastors especially, I feel you struggling with your flesh. You feel God leading you in a clear direction, but then you think, "That's not how you're supposed to have church."

*PLEASE SHOW ME THE RULE BOOK ON HOW YOU'RE SUPPOSED TO HAVE CHURCH!*

Please show me the rule book on how you're supposed to have church? Please show me, in the Word, where we should have 20 minutes of praise and worship, five minutes of announcements, 30 minutes of tithes and offering collection, and then a 40 minute message?

# Finding Balance

Don't you think it's time to separate tradition from mandate and just get down to business?

However, before we knock it, realize that there is a place for tradition, too.

My grandparents attended the same church for over 22 years. They served in the Bible study right into my grandfather's 90s. I've never seen two warriors of God as sharp in the Word as them, being a blessing right where they were.

I remember going to that church when I was a little girl, bored out of my mind. I love them dearly, but man, that wasn't my tribe. Yet, I looked at them, and I saw the influence they had right where they were.

I thank God for that church family who continues to reach people in that community. Am I going to walk in such a church and say, "Okay guys, we need flat screen TVs and a smoke machine? Come now, catch up with the times."

Why should I?

That's not their mandate. Can we stop imposing on one another? We talk about having unity in the body of Christ. We'll have that unity when we stop imposing our mandate on others.

Craig and I've been so blessed to be sent to so many of these groups. We've met hidden warriors, who are called to specific realms within their workplace.

# International Positioning

God sent His apostles internationally. He has sent people from Africa to Germany to reach the Germans within the workplace. Talk about a switch-around! He didn't send them to start a church or ministry, but rather to become an influence from within the marketplace!

They went underground. And in that darkness, the glory of the Lord came on them. It's here that kings will be drawn to the brightness of your rising. If you're one of those seeds that God sent into the darkness, the glory is coming. It's time.

> *IF YOU'RE ONE OF THOSE SEEDS THAT GOD HAS SENT INTO THE DARKNESS, THE GLORY IS COMING. IT'S TIME.*

When I step back a little and look at the broad picture, I realize how small each of us are. I also realize that if we each build on our land, we'll establish the Kingdom.

We'll have a kingdom of cities, tribes, and clans. God has a place just for you. If you've a fire burning in you that's diverse and cuts against the grain — you're not alone. There are many mighty warriors, just like you, called to the impossible.

I'm privileged to know many of these new breed of apostles, and am truly humbled by their journey. These are our unspoken heroes of which you could be one.

# 3

# THE SLEEPER APOSTLES

With every shifting sand, the Lord set your feet on the land He designed for you to build on. Now the movement has begun, and your comfort zone is being rocked. Don't be concerned. The Lord is waking you! The spotlight has begun to shine on the hidden warriors. Don't look for them on the million dollar platforms.

Seek them out in the darkest of places. Seek them out in the trenches with dirty hands and a weight on their backs. Apostles and mighty leaders of God doing what God has called them to do regardless of whether the thousands flock to their message or not!

## JOSEPH

These apostles are like Joseph. I'm trying to determine if God punished or blessed Joseph by giving him a vision of what would come? He showed Joseph the stars and sheaves bowing to him. (Genesis 37)

"Wow! Look at what God is going to do! I'm going to change the world! I'm going to rise up in the public eye."

Instead of glory he lost his coat of many colors.

There comes a time when you think, "This is a bit of a setback, but I'm sure it will get better soon. Look, I have a new job position with this guy named Potiphar. He trusts me with everything - my time to shine is just around the corner."

Pity about Potiphar's wife. Joseph didn't know how to work those politics. He was falsely accused, fell from favor, and landed in prison.

You rise up, you fall. You rise up, you fall. You think, "God, that night when you gave me the vision - was that really you? That night as I laid on my bed and you told me your plans... where is that God, as I sit alone in prison?"

## The Price: You're Not Allowed "Normal"

These apostles were sent into the world. They weren't allowed to rise up in the Church. God had them focus on their careers. It was never what they wanted to do and was never their fire.

> THESE APOSTLES WERE SENT INTO THE WORLD. THEY WEREN'T ALLOWED TO RISE UP IN THE CHURCH.

I call these the Sleeper Apostles. It's an underground movement. God sent His agents into every system of this world. Perhaps you're in the military, healthcare system, political system, entertainment system, or the marketplace.

You're pushing through with your career and waiting for God to release you so that you can finally do His work. Child of God, has it ever occurred to you that this is your call? You are a sleeper, and you're waiting for your time to be activated.

*YOU ARE A SLEEPER, AND YOU'RE WAITING FOR YOUR TIME TO BE ACTIVATED.*

I'm here to tell you that the time is now! God will use you from within the system. God didn't raise Joseph out of prison to then send him back home. He put the man on the throne. God elevated him right within Pharaoh's kingdom, to take a seat next to the king, and so save his people.

# ESTHER AND MORDECAI

> ***Esther 2:10*** *Esther had not revealed her people or family, for Mordecai had charged her not to reveal it.*

Look at Esther and Mordecai! Was their process and positioning any easier?

Esther travailed. She said, "How can I do this? I'm a Jew."

Mordecai said, "Don't say anything about your nationality."

"How can I take this position in the world? I'm a Christian. I don't even believe what this political party believes. I'm in here trying to fight for a cause that seems to be so against what I stand for. What am I doing in the world, in politics? What am I doing here?"

Mordecai said, "Hold your peace. God knows what He is doing."

When the time came, Esther saved her nation. God has you there for a reason. Talk about a conspiracy theory! God has been at work. He has planted His secret agents in the systems of the world for years.

> GOD HAS BEEN AT WORK. HE HAS PLANTED HIS SECRET AGENTS IN THE SYSTEMS OF THE WORLD FOR YEARS.

Unbelievers won't need to go to churches to get saved any longer. You will find them in key places, all over the world. If you're one God has seemed to shut up and send out, you're exactly where He needs you to be.

## You Are Not Alone

Very soon, those doors will open. Again, you're not alone. God is there with you. When you look to the left and right in the spirit, you'll see that there are many others like you.

For those of you who feel it's a sin to have a church in Hollywood, or to dabble in politics, you're not alone. I'm preaching to myself here. Us prophetic types view the world through eyes that see in only black and white.

"That is sin. Touch not the unclean thing!"

I used to say things like, "There is no place for Christians in politics! There is no place for Christians in the stock market - that's the devil and his work!"

Well, how else will we have some kind of dominion in this earth?

## Diversity of Mandates

Joseph rose up in Egypt, which is a picture of the world. He used the resources of Egypt to save his people. Why can't we do the same? Let's not be high-minded and judge our brothers because they carry an anointing that doesn't agree with ours!

## Dial Down the Judgment

When you receive a mandate, much like Joseph did, it consumes you. Come now, Apostle, you know what I'm talking about. It's your baby. You taste it, smell it, feel it, and see it. It becomes who you are.

Somebody on the outside doesn't get it. They have a different mandate that they're consumed by. So, don't assume that just because you don't understand it that it's not of God.

It's time to allow the Holy Spirit to redirect our thinking. It's also time to come out of hiding and to stand up boldly!

There are others with the same passion who will be drawn to the brightness of your rising. However, if you're not bold enough to declare it, how will they ever know that you're there?

God is not releasing just one mandate to the Church.

I hear things like, "The Lord is raising up the Joshuas in this season."

I wait around for the rest of the message but nope... that's it.

"The Lord is releasing the Elijah anointing."

I think, "Yeah, that was 15 years ago. Is that it?"

"The Esthers are arising..."

## SMASHING LIMITATIONS ON YOUR MANDATE

We're so narrow-minded. We think that God has this bag and He just pulls out one anointing at a time.

"Just one anointing for you this year, Church."

"I have a lot of callings, anointings, and ministries, but this year... it's just the Esthers. If you're an Elijah, Solomon, or another type, then you're going to have to wait until next year!

I'm thinking to myself here, if the Lord only releases one anointing a year, I'm going to die before mine is released!

Can we step back and see the broad view? We need to realize that we are meant to establish the Kingdom of God in this earth, and to do that, we need many generals, commanders, different kinds of churches, leaders, and mandates.

## ANOINTING REQUIRED

All of these mandates are also going to require different kinds of anointings.

*GOD IS RELEASING A FLOOD OF DIVERSITY IN ANOINTING, MANDATE, AND FUNCTION. FIND YOURS!*

If you run after every anointing each year, you'll become really tired, really fast. God is releasing a flood of diverse anointings, mandates, and functions. Find yours!

Find your land and build on it. When Moses divided the land between the children of Israel, he was particular. Benjamin didn't traipse over to Judah's land and set up camp.

The tribe of Issachar didn't fight for Manasseh's land because they thought it was greener on the other side.

They stuck to their allocated land. In fact, even when the Israelites married, they had to make sure that the land stayed within its allocated tribe. However, you want to go around collecting all the anointings and mandates, wondering which one is yours.

You cling to the hem of every garment you find, asking, "Is this one mine?"

Why don't you just ask God? Why don't you ask Him which land He has given you, instead of looking at everyone else's land and saying that you like that better?

God has not run out of land. If there is no anointing or mandate that fits you, God can give you one. He is not running out any time soon. He brought you into this earth for a reason. You have a specific purpose.

Don't feel like you're losing out if you're not in on the latest church trend. Maybe you're not meant to be in on the latest trend. God has a land that's suited just for you. Find it, build upon it, and establish it. Then, you're going to start seeing some miracles.

# 4

# Your Process to Discovering the "More"

*1 Corinthians 13:9 For we know in part and we prophesy in part.*
*10 But when that which is perfect has come, then that which is in part will be done away.*

It took years to develop in the anointings, gifts of the Spirit, and the character traits you have.

Your circumstantial pressures had a single purpose. God designed them to bring you to where you are today. However, when that which is perfect has come, that which is in part shall be done away.

Labor with me a little bit. Your spiritual gifts, anointings, the people you ministered to, and your disappointments all positioned you for today.

We're so foolish. We receive an anointing or a spiritual gift, and we cling to it for dear life. The Lord knows that we had to fast, pray, beg, and plead to get it! Then we finally get it and forget that it was "in part".

God always had a bigger plan for you. All of that experience had one purpose. It led you to this point. Here is the good news - you're at another point of transition in your apostolic walk. This is what the transition looks like: It's time to release what brought you to this point. You cannot go into your new land with it.

> YOU ARE AT ANOTHER POINT OF TRANSITION IN YOUR APOSTOLIC WALK.

Why?

## Embrace the Transition

Because its purpose is expired. Time to transition! You have a greater mandate to carry. If you're going to build, then you've to learn building skills. You need a new anointing and ability.

You need a new character trait. If you try to establish the land that God has given you today, with the anointings of yesterday, you'll fall flat on your face.

> IF YOU TRY TO ESTABLISH THE LAND THAT GOD HAS GIVEN YOU TODAY, WITH THE ANOINTINGS OF YESTERDAY, YOU'LL FALL FLAT ON YOUR FACE.

There is nothing more terrifying than to stand up to do what you've always done, with the anointing you've always had, but it just doesn't work... it's outright broken!

## Did I Just Lose My Anointing?

"When I laid hands on the sick, they recovered. When I prayed for finances, they flowed. When I preached, the tears of healing flowed."

That which is in part shall be done away when that which is perfect has come.

*THAT WHICH IS IN PART SHALL BE DONE AWAY WHEN THAT WHICH IS PERFECT HAS COME.*

This is not a sign that you've failed God. It's a sign that you're in position for a new mandate.

Let it go! God has so much more for you. He has a new anointing for you.

You went to preach the message that you always did, and it fell flat. Here is why - It was in part. Let it go and discard it like an old pair of shoes and get some new ones!

Can I please break your limited thinking? Would you please allow me to smash the way that you perceive yourself and your call?

Why don't you allow Him to stretch you a little?

## Shift a Little!

> **Philippians 3:13** *Brethren, I don't count myself to have apprehended; but one thing I do, forgetting those things which are behind and reaching forward to those things which are ahead,*

**14** *I press toward the goal for the prize of the upward call of God in Christ Jesus.*

If you're a pastor, can the Lord transition you into the prophetic? Why not? Can God do that, or have you boxed Him in and told Him what He can and cannot do in your life?

So, you've always been poor. Good, you should do business then. You have always done business. Good, you should learn to minister in the arts.

"But God has given me an anointing for business."

No, you studied at business school. That is where you got your "anointing" for business. Allow God to give you something that comes from the scrolls of heaven and not the libraries of man.

It delights me to be able to say, as Paul said in Philippians, "I don't boast because of all the things that I had. I left them behind and pressed forward toward Christ."

You end up doing things that you never knew were in you, because they weren't in you. He put them in you. Didn't you know that God can put skill, business plans, arts, creativity, and wisdom in you?

## The Solomon Model

David was a man of war.

During his time there were still some unconquered territories from the time of Joshua. Some territories were lost through various wars. So, along comes David was a man of war and blood, with a heart that was the same as God's. He stepped up to the plate and took those territories back.

He established a pattern for the Temple and a pattern for 24-hour praise and worship. I want to look a little further now. Solomon did something that none of the judges or the kings before him did. While Moses established a nation, Solomon established a kingdom.

> WHILE MOSES ESTABLISHED A NATION, SOLOMON ESTABLISHED A KINGDOM.

Let me show you how he established this kingdom.

> ***2 Chronicles 8:1*** *It came to pass at the end of twenty years, when Solomon had built the house of the Lord and his own house,*
> *2 that the cities which Hiram had given to Solomon, Solomon built them; and he settled the children of Israel there.*
> *3 And Solomon went to Hamath Zobah and seized it.*
> *4 He also built Tadmor in the wilderness, and all the storage cities which he built in Hamath.*
> *5 He built Upper Beth Horon and Lower Beth Horon, fortified cities with walls, gates, and bars,*
> *6 Also Baalath and all the storage cities that Solomon had, and all the chariot cities and the cities of the cavalry, and all that Solomon desired to build in Jerusalem, in Lebanon, and in all the land of his dominion.*
> *7 All the people who were left of the Hittites, Amorites, Perizzites, Hivites, and Jebusites, who weren't of Israel -*
> *8 That is, their descendants who were left in the land*

*after them, whom the children of Israel didn't destroy - from these Solomon raised forced labor, as it's to this day.*

Solomon was a builder. How did he establish the pattern? He did it by establishing the land. He built the Temple, his palace, and city after city.

When I read this scripture, I found it fascinating how each city was diverse, yet so specific in its function. One city, Tadmor, was built just for commerce. This was like an oasis in the middle of the wilderness.

Right next to it, he built a storage city, which was smart to have near a city of commerce. Then, he built a chariot city and a cavalry city. Think about that! He had a city just for chariots and another just for storehouses.

What a beautiful picture of where God wants to take us as a Church. We'll diversify, but first, we need to build.

It was because Solomon built on the land that he established it. The Word says that this was Israel's wealthiest season. Bronze was considered garbage in his time. Do you know why? It was because Solomon didn't just establish his ministry. He built on the land, and the children of Israel came to dwell in it.

> IT WAS BECAUSE SOLOMON BUILT ON THE LAND THAT HE ESTABLISHED IT.

## Do More Than "Go Into Ministry"

"I'm going into ministry, stand behind the pulpit and preach the Word of God."

What will your city be when you die? Will you leave a city behind for others to dwell in?

*SOLOMON DIDN'T MAKE THE PEOPLE RICH BY GIVING THEM ALL OF HIS MONEY. HE MADE THEM RICH BY BUILDING CITIES.*

Solomon didn't make the people rich by giving them all of his money. He made them rich by building cities, putting them into those cities, and teaching them how to take care of themselves. They became wealthy from their own labor.

We have to build the land that God gave us. We cannot continue just going from one level to the next. We have to build what we already have.

Take the relationships you have. The ministry opportunities, people and environment you're in, and make it work. Rock it and make it amazing! Become strong and allow yourself to be expanded upon!

**Stop trying to shoot higher and begin building deeper**

There will always be future ministry visions. God is not done with you yet, but what are you doing with what you have today?

*STOP TRYING TO SHOOT HIGHER AND START BUILDING DEEPER.*

God has given you one pulpit and one ministry opportunity. God has given you a small group, but you're saying, "One day, when I have a megachurch..."

If that's how you think all the time, then you're never going to reach the people that are in front of you today. Solomon did better than that. He didn't just see how he could be the greatest king that ever lived.

He looked around and said, "Lord, I need wisdom. This is a great people. Help me to help your people."

He built them cities, but he didn't live in them. Once he had built them, he went back home. Change your ministry focus!

## Revolutionize Your Perspective

We always think that we'll build up our ministries, but there are many who will be called to build ministries for others and then walk away. You will build cities for other people to live in. And so, you'll be extending the Kingdom of God!

It's time to build on your promised land. You won land with every battle you won. You and I both know that you could've fought a little harder sometimes. Some of us even received land that we didn't want.

Solomon gave Hiram portions of land that weren't well received. So Solomon took them back and built them into cities. It's not what your land looks like, it's what you do with it that matters.

*IT'S NOT WHAT YOUR LAND LOOKS LIKE, IT'S WHAT YOU DO WITH IT THAT MATTERS.*

"If only I had the opportunities that Pastor Joe down the road had, then I would have an amazing ministry."

Why don't you just take what you have, instead of being discontented?

Be discontent with the state of the Church! Be discontent with the fact that Jesus is not ruling and reigning over every system of the world yet! Let's be discontent with that.

Then let us be content with the portion and the talent that God has put in our hands and start to use it, multiply it, and grow it so that we can be accountable to His plan.

# 5

# APOSTOLIC TYPES IN THE MOVEMENT

In this season, we'll have a variety of apostolic types to fulfill various mandates. The first one that I will talk about is David. I like to call him a couple of things. I like to see him as a worshiper, trainer, and team builder. My favorite title for him though is, "The Tradition Breaker".

## DAVID – THE TRADITION BREAKER

He is going to leave the traditional church system. He is a trainer of mighty men by nature. He has eyes to see the mighty men that nobody else does. He can walk into a meeting or a church, see the hidden warriors and pull them out to engage in war.

However, he cannot change the Church from within. David sure tried though, just like you.

You tried a staid church, and you tried to play the choirboy, but that didn't work out for you, did it?

"What is wrong with me? I'm so done with tradition and religion!"

God sends you out into the Cave of Adullam to train your mighty men. It's because you're a David. It's because David went out and trained his mighty men that he could establish Jerusalem as the city of the king.

He established 24-hour praise and worship. He put the Ark of the Covenant back in place and designed the pattern for Solomon to build by. With his commanders appointed, he established a military structure that had not existed before.

Yet, he could not stay within the kingdom to do it. He had to go out. It's the same with those who have such a mandate. Other people will be permitted to function within the status quo, but not you.

> OTHER PEOPLE WILL BE PERMITTED TO FUNCTION WITHIN THE STATUS QUO, BUT NOT YOU.

## Joseph – The Undercover Businessman

Joseph was hidden until it was his time. They're called to the systems of this world. Some call them marketplace apostles.

They are called to commerce. The frustrating part is the conflict within. Such apostles struggle with the world and the Church, the Lord and their career, the call and wanting to make money.

"You are such a heathen, pagan, and sinner, because you want to make money!"

It turns out that Joseph had a head for it. He made Pharaoh incredibly rich by the end of his mandate.

I won't delve into the righteousness or unrighteousness of mammon. That's not what this chapter is about. I just want you to know that I've met and seen those in the Church who are called to be Josephs.

God made them down in the church. They had no choice but to rise up through the world system, surrounded and smothered by the world, until they were sick of the taste of the world. Yet, God still would not release them.

Your time is coming. God has put that fire in you for a purpose. We see them already. Open your eyes. They're everywhere.

## ESTHER AND MORDECAI – POLITICAL KINGDOM CHANGERS

Next, we have Esther and Mordecai. They're the ones who touch the unclean thing. You either love them or hate them, but yet, they're radically changing the political landscape from within.

*GOD HAS POSITIONED LEADERS IN THE POLITICAL SYSTEM. I LOVE HOW THEY'RE A THORN IN SATAN'S SIDE.*

Agree or disagree bit it doesn't change the fact that God has positioned leaders in the political system. I love how they're a thorn in satan's side.

They're a stone in his shoe. He tries to run in a certain direction, and then here comes an annoying politician who sticks him in his heel. Get ready for it! Things will become very uncomfortable for the enemy.

God has position his leaders in the judicial system, to ensure His plan is set in motion. They see with eyes we don't. I cannot say that I always agree with their stance.

Sometimes I look at these guys and I'm divided on whether God or their political agenda take preeminence in their lives. However, I won't judge because I see that they're mandated by God. I cannot deny the fruit of their labor. I see God moving within their circles, so I respect that.

It's natural to feel confused about the apostolic mandate of others. We're each given a territory. I know my territory and am comfortable in it. I know every mountain and ravine of it. So naturally, Esther and Mordecai's territory is foreign to me. However, just because it's foreign doesn't mean it's wrong. It doesn't mean my mandate is of greater or less importance. This is a movement – not a stream.

This is a movement, not a circle. This goes beyond the boundaries of your norm.

Then I must concede that they may look at me with my big mouth and say, "She would make a terrible politician." They might not comprehend that a woman can be an apostle. They might not feel comfortable with the concept of spiritual parenting. Does that make what I do wrong?

It's only when you have the maturity to recognize the mandate others walk in, that the uniqueness of yours becomes clear.

We each have our part to play in the body of Christ.

## NEHEMIAH – LEADERS OF THE PROPHETIC MOVEMENT

Nehemiah's have the passion to equip prophetic warriors. Nehemiah surveyed the walls and gathered everyone to build, with a sword in one hand and a trowel in the other.

They're prophetic apostles. Leaders of the prophetic movement. Nehemiah apostles are assembling the prophets to birth the prophetic move and then to protect it.

> NEHEMIAH APOSTLES ARE ASSEMBLING THE PROPHETS TO BIRTH THE PROPHETIC MOVE AND THEN TO PROTECT IT.

We were the first online prophetic school in 1999. It was revolutionary. If you looked up prophetic school in those days, you found us at the top of the page. There weren't a whole lot of prophets being trained online yet.

Today online prophetic schools are a dime a dozen and I'm thrilled to see it! We need the prophets mobilized.

I see the Nehemiah's assembling the prophets to take their place.

If you've been called as a prophet but have a fire to see prophets mobilized, then it could well be that you're a Nehemiah.

Read the book of Nehemiah and seek God on your mandate. Then, get ready to put your hand to the trowel because there's a lot of work to be done.

## EZRA – CHURCH AND MINISTRY PLANTERS

> ***Ezra 9:9 (NKJV)*** *"For we were slaves. Yet our God did not forsake us in our bondage; but He extended mercy to us in the sight of the kings of Persia, to revive us, to repair the house of our God, to rebuild its ruins, and to give us a wall in Judah and Jerusalem."*

The last one I will mention is Ezra. Ezra built the Temple. There are many other apostolic types that I will leave for a book focused on the subject.

Ezra wasn't content to pore over the pattern of the Temple. He wanted to build it. Ezra apostles don't just have an idea of what the Temple should look like - they're anointed to build it.

They're the guys who found the business churches, arts churches, and so forth.

They're builders. They don't just prophesy about it. They put their hands in the soil, mobilize the forces, and plant churches. They found ministries of every kind.

When you read Ezra and Nehemiah, you'll note that these calls come with opposition. The world will try to crush you to stop the work. Don't make the mistake of thinking that because there's opposition, that you're not being led.

*PAY ATTENTION THOUGH, JUST BECAUSE THERE IS OPPOSITION, DOESN'T MEAN THAT YOU'RE NOT LED.*

It's convenient to say, "If it was of God, everything would fall into place."

"If it was of God, we would not face this opposition."

"Everything went wrong, and this is a sign that we should not build."

That's not what Ezra or Nehemiah thought. They didn't say that it was a sign from God that they shouldn't build. They knew where the opposition came from!

It's not a sign from God that you should stop building. It's a sign from the enemy that he is afraid of what you're building, and it's time to pick up your sword and trowel once again and to take this land.

> IT'S NOT A SIGN FROM GOD THAT YOU SHOULD STOP BUILDING. IT'S A SIGN FROM THE ENEMY THAT HE IS AFRAID OF WHAT YOU'RE BUILDING.

## What Land Is Yours?

Let me stretch you a bit. What has God done in the last couple of months? What unexpected shifts have you experienced?

Look at your marriage and social environment. Did God cut off any old relationships? Did He add any new relationships to you?

What about ministry opportunities? Has God opened new ones and closed down others?

For business and work, you may have had hopes and dreams. You thought you'd accomplish great things but God shut the door. Then, He opened a door to something completely out of your depth! Now you have no idea what to do. It's not your first choice. In fact, that land might even be an "over my dead body" kind of choice!

It sounds to me like you've gained yourself some land. When that which is perfect has come, that which is in part shall be done away. It's time to allow those old doors and opportunities that God cut off and let them die.

## Making the Relationship Transition

I especially feel this regarding relationships. There are some relationships that God has cut off, but you're trying so hard to re-establish them. You feel obligated and guilty. Listen, if God wants to fix it, He will.

(I'm speaking of relationships other than marriage. Marriage conflict requires counsel and an external perspective.)

The Lord may have removed a son, daughter, father, mother, aunt, uncle, or friend. You fight Him because it doesn't seem like "the right thing to do." God knows what He's doing.

If you don't let go, you'll hinder their walk, and they'll hinder yours. You need to step forward. I'm not saying that you won't connect again further down the road, but right now, this land doesn't include them.

Let it go! Let the old land go! Let the old anointing go! Let the old visions die!

## Watching Your Promises Burn

God had me do something unexpected.

For years, every time God gave me a promise in a journal or through the Word, I would write them down and date them. I had a collection of promises that I would meditate on day and night, like Joshua did.

As I was preparing for the new year, the Lord said, "The sand is about to shift beneath your feet."

I thought, "I get that. Die already. I know the drill."

Then He said, "You know all of those promises that I've given you through the years?"

"Yes, Lord."

"Go to that file and delete them. I want you to delete them whether they came to pass or not."

It was an emotional moment for me. I went to my app where I kept all my promises, and I went through them one by one and deleted them. One painful line at a time.

I was surprised. As I went through those promises, I saw many that had come to pass. Often though they hadn't come to pass the way I had expected them to.

What shook me most though was this. Even though many of those promises had come to pass, I kept looking back on them as if they hadn't. I now saw that list for what it was: A collection of promises that kept me looking back.

For a season, they propelled me toward destiny and kept me going, hoping, and dreaming.

The Lord said, "All of my promises brought you to this point. Now, that which is in part must be done away so that which is perfect can come. Colette, let the promises go!"

The hardest ones to let go of were the ones that were unfulfilled. This was especially true for the ones where I felt that I had failed.

It wasn't hard because the promise was hard to let go of. It was hard because I felt responsible for failing.

The Lord comforted me, "Even your failure and inability has brought you to this point. Do you think I didn't know what would happen?

> IT'S A NEW SEASON! I'VE MANY NEW PROMISES FOR YOU, WHICH I CANNOT GIVE YOU WHILE YOU'RE HOLDING ONTO THE OLD ONES.

It's a new season! I've many new promises for you, which I cannot give you while you're holding onto the old ones. So, don't be like Lot's wife, looking back at the old promises and the old land."

Take all of your accomplishments, trophies, failures, regrets, hopes, dreams, and desires, and put them on the altar.

I imagine what it was like for the children of Israel to finally walk into their inheritance. They had been in the wilderness, and known the taste of manna. Now, there they stood, having won the land.

They were ready to establish their first house and raise a family. How must it have felt for them?

## Adjusting from the Wilderness Mentality to Prosperity

I can imagine that it took some adjustment. They were accustomed to perpetual war. They were used to fighting for survival. They were so used to pushing and struggling, to the point that this concept of raising a family, building a house and a vegetable garden, and having a normal life, must have felt foreign to them.

They needed to change the way they thought. In the same way you to need to change the way that you think. What you don't realize is that this is the ultimate warfare.

There is the warfare that we engage in when we take the land and pray it through. We bind the enemy, stand in faith, and get the victory.

Then there is apostolic warfare. This is one where we build upon that land and put Jesus as the king upon it. We put His flag on the tower of that land.

We walk into the enemy's camp and into the systems of the world to hold our flag high. This is the kind of warfare that allows Jesus to rule and reign in this land. It means building and establishing His name in all the earth.

# 6

# YOU ARE THE CHURCH

***Colossians 3:1-2*** *If then you were raised with Christ, seek those things which are above, where Christ is, sitting at the right hand of God. Set your mind on things above, not on things on the earth.*

We stand in an incredible time. I cannot contain my excitement, because I feel so privileged to be part of what God is doing with us! It's easy to let what's happening in the world sidetrack us. However, take a moment to set your sights on what God has in mind.

We get to see what generations before us never did. We'll participate in something that they could only dream of. Years ago, they received the dream and the promise, but we get to see the promise fulfilled.

*YEARS AGO, THEY RECEIVED THE DREAM AND THE PROMISE, BUT WE GET TO SEE THE PROMISE FULFILLED.*

Additionally, God has given us the privilege of participating and bringing that promise to pass. It won't be one person, one apostle, or one ministry that will usher in this apostolic move.

Together, as leaders, we'll combine our pieces of the blueprint to build the master's plan!

Is that so hard to imagine? It's was just as hard to imagine for the Early Church. They saw something being birthed dreamed about for generations.

They waited for their Messiah. They prayed for their revival to come, but when it came, it came in a way that they didn't anticipate. It came with greater power than they anticipated.

So, we stand on a threshold in this new Church era. We feel the trembling under our feet. Every time our prophets get together to pray, we feel the move of the Spirit. We feel the heart of the Father, and His heart is beating faster. We know that this earth is in travail, waiting for us to take a step forward.

So, why have these promises not come to pass? If God has given these promises so many years ago, why has it taken so long for them to come to pass?

## Why Has Revival Tarried?

When the children of Israel left Egypt, the Lord brought them to their Promised Land. The land flowing with milk and honey was within their grasp. What happened? Moses sent out spies. They looked at the Promised Land and said, "Yes, it's true. The land that God has promised us is indeed rich and beautiful."

However, the price that God asked them to pay for that land was more than they were willing to pay. The giants were too big, the warfare was too intense, the opposition was too much. They came back grumbling, instead of trusting the Almighty God who promised them that land.

They could've trusted the Lord to bring about the miracle needed to take that land. Instead, they took one look at the price and declared it was too high.

They missed their time of visitation. Then, the Lord said, "I will wait for a new generation to come." Then, they suddenly woke up from their slumber and thought to take that land in their own strength.

They said, "God will be with us!" Their newfound faith born more out of fear of loss than true belief. So, they tried again to take the land... but we know what happened after that.

## The Journey

Read Numbers 14, and you'll see what happened.

> THEY TRIED TO TAKE HOLD OF GOD'S PROMISE THE WORLD'S WAY.

They tried to take hold of God's promise the world's way. They had the same results as when they ran away from paying the price in the first place.

It's the same with you. God gives you a promise, and then you think, "Lord, that's a high price to pay. Do I have to give up my job, relationships, and comfort zones? Those are some big giants.

Let me tell you, Lord, what price I'm willing to pay. I'm willing to fast, to study, to pick up my sword and shield and go into battle in your name. That is what I'm willing to do in order to fulfill the promise that you've given me. I'm willing to preach from the pulpit. I'm willing to lead a crusade in your honor."

Who would have anticipated that God's idea of taking the land was to walk around the walls until they fell? If only they would've waited on God a little bit longer instead of complaining. They would've found out that God had a much simpler way of bringing down those giants than they imagined.

We see that parallel in the Church today.

## Complete Segregation

As the Church faced persecution we see two reactions.

First, the Church said, "Look at all those giants in the world. We cannot compare to the world. We're not good enough. We don't match up, so we'll separate ourselves.

The Church will be on one mountain, and the world will be on the other. Then the Church 'must not touch' the unholy thing.

We have Sunday meetings and Wednesday bible studies with pleasant times of fellowship. We sit in our Christian-based support group and the only guy who steps out of its walls is the evangelist. He's the lone ranger who's sent to venture over to the "world mountain." His instruction being that once he's snagged a few to drag all those sinners back to the "Church mountain".

That was the pattern for the Church, and then God started shaking it up. The apostolic move began, and we shifted our perspective.

"If we want to win the lost, why don't we camp on their mountain? Why don't we all carry the message of salvation, instead of leaving it all to the evangelist?"

A revolution took place in the Church. We saw healing revivalists and Pentecostal revivalists sprouting up everywhere. We finally got the message that not everyone on the world mountain was going to come knocking on our door to be saved.

## THE SPIRIT OF THE WORLD

Then, we also saw another extreme. There were parts of the Church that thought, "We had a bit of success, so why don't we take up our swords and shields, just like we see the world doing, and imitate them?

If we want our numbers to grow, we need to become more acceptable to the world. If we want to pack those pews, we need to sound like the world, look like the world, and act like the world.

At the same time, we'll still keep our message of grace. The change will be the change in our hearts and people will see that we are good, moral people, and they'll ask us about Christ. If we want to get people from the world mountain to ours, we need to rebuild until we have an environment that makes them comfortable."

We know what happened. Lukewarm, seeker-friendly Christianity came into its own.

Now, when you look at the Church's mountain and the world's mountain, you ponder, "Which one is which again? I cannot tell because the world has better charities than the Church. Oftentimes the world preaches a better moral code than the Church."

So, what makes us different again?

# The Church of the Future

All this time, we wait for the Lord to step in with His power and shake the walls of Jericho on our behalf. Are we ready to finally do things God's way?

Are we prepared to face our giants and to take them down as God wants us to?

> *ARE WE PREPARED TO FACE OUR GIANTS AND TO TAKE THEM DOWN AS GOD WANTS US TO?*

## A Church Without Walls

God is establishing a Church without walls. I'm not talking about a Church where you spread the gospel among the prostitutes and in bars. (This is certainly a powerful ministry, but not the exact concept I'm expounding on.)

I'm talking about a Church where the Church stops being a building and starts becoming a body. I'm talking about the Church being a person.

I'm talking about people saying, "We're going to the church next door," and they mean they're going to fellowship with their neighbors.

I'm talking about a Church that's a living, breathing organism, and not a brick-and-mortar building where we all go and fellowship on Sunday. It's been flogged to death by every preacher who wants all members to return to church on Sunday, "Forsake not the fellowship of the saints."

Well, we should be fellowshipping every day. We should be walking out our Christianity every day.

As apostles, we should be declaring, "Look at me, people! I'm a living, breathing Church. This is what the Church looks like. You are what the Church looks like."

The Church should be scattered within the world. Let's banish having two mountains and compromising so that we look like the world. I'm talking about a trendsetting Church where the world follows after our example. A dynamic where we set the standards.

# 7

# A TRENDSETTING CHURCH

***Matthew 5:14 (NKJV)*** *"You are the light of the world. A city that is set on a hill cannot be hidden."*

We should be what the world attains to. Yes, we had the one extreme, "Touch not the world," and we were so separated that we could not watch TV or listen to the radio because it was of the devil. We restricted the good news from those who were dying and needed it most.

However, now we have the opposite extreme. Jesus is coming for a spotless bride, but His bride is contaminated with the spirit of the world. Ministries are hunting for lighting from Las Vegas so that they can have a lit stage.

The thinking permeating the church sounds like, "We have to look like the world and act like the world in order to reach the world."

So, what spirit is in the Church?

I feel the heart of the Father, the travail in the spirit. I hear the cry of intercession for the prophets to rise up and start decreeing the word to shake the Church and wake the Church, because... you're the Church!

# You Are the City on a Hill

Stop waiting for someone else to make things happen. You are the Church. If anything is going to happen, that change will start with you because God has called you to be a city on a hill.

You are to be a model wherever you may be. Wherever you work, wherever you socialize, wherever you study, be an example for others to follow.

God is scattering the Church and breaking down our buildings. He is breaking down that city on the mountain and making all of us into mountains and cities.

> *GOD WANTS US TO BE MORE THAN A CITY ON THE HILL. HE WANTS US TO BE A KINGDOM.*

God wants us to be more than a city on the hill. He wants us to be a Kingdom.

He is lighting each of us with a fire directly from His heart. All we need to do is find our place and become the light in the darkness. What was the great commission? To go forth into all the world and make disciples of all men. (Matthew 28:19)

I love the wording. It doesn't say that we are to go evangelize everyone. It says that we are to make disciples of them. The Scriptures on the great commission share the same wording: To disciple, to teach, to instruct!

What happens when you're a mentor? It means that what is in you, is imparted to the person you're mentoring.

Visualize with me a Church where every believer with the Spirit of Christ is the teacher, the boss, the leader, the example, and the model. Imagine that we were the one others look to for direction, counsel, guidance, education, and business information.

## A Church of Influence and Power

Imagine a Church where the world is continually being influenced by on-fire believers. However, that's not what we're seeing. We're seeing the Church scurry like little mice, trying to get a piece of cheese from the world.

Then, they bring that stale, contaminated cheese back to the church building, and they poison everyone with it. That is not what God has for us. So why then, Apostle, are you so surprised that the Lord is shaking things up? Are you still convinced that it's the enemy trying to steal your right as a believer to gather or worship the Lord?

Visualize with me for a moment - Apostle Paul who persecuted the Early Church, and so was instrumental to birthing Antioch. In the same way, consider that what we deem as persecution in our Church era is in fact the hand of God to fulfill His purpose.

> WHAT WE DEEM AS PERSECUTION IN OUR CHURCH ERA IS IN FACT THE HAND OF GOD TO FULFILL HIS PURPOSE.

I've seen the Lord pick up leaders, believers, and fivefold ministers and scatter them. I've seen the Lord take well-structured ministries away from an apostle. He then took that same apostle and thrust them into the workplace.

"Okay, Lord. You have called me to the work of the ministry, right?"

"Yes, I have."

"You have called me to be an apostle, right?"

"Yes, I have."

"Then, why did you take my ministry away (or have me give it away!)? It seems a little counterproductive."

"I took it away because this new territory is your ministry. You are meant to be a church in the world. Go and excel there! Shine your light there, and I will draw many men unto you."

## BREAKING MINISTRY MINDSETS

Ministry is not just about standing on a platform. Let's get practical about this for a minute, okay?

God has made it clear to many who have a fivefold ministry calling that He's raising a Church where every believer is a light in the darkness. His desire is for every believer to walk in their call.

Sounds fantastic, right? However, if we try to stick to our old ministry mindsets, how will we find enough pulpits for everyone? There are so many meetings in a month, guys! If every believer in the Church is activated to fulfill their call, the pastor is never going to get a word in at Sunday service!

I'm playing on the point realizing how foolish it sounds. But for many, doing the work of the ministry still revolves around having podium time.

There's so much more to ministry we haven't even tapped into.

God is removing our complacency.

The apostolic movement is multi-directional. It's coming upon us in waves from every single direction. It's touching every denomination and every nation.

It's not only America, or Africa, Canada, or Europe that will be blessed. God is moving His hand in a way that He never has before. This is not a single wave.

I'm talking about whirlpools all over the world. I'm talking about believers taking their place and recognizing their call in the workplace, in education, in politics, in the world, in psychology... everywhere!

The Church hasn't touched these systems nearly enough. I should know because I used to be the one preaching "touch not the unholy thing". Well, if no believer touches the unholy thing, guess what happens? It remains unholy.

*WELL, IF NO BELIEVER TOUCHES THE UNHOLY THING, GUESS WHAT HAPPENS? IT REMAINS UNHOLY.*

God has put you where you are for purpose. However, we are sitting and waiting for miracles to happen. We're saying, "Lord, I will step out and do your work when the miracle takes place."

However, the Lord is saying, "No. When you step out, then you'll see the miracle."

# THE KING'S ADVISORS

Where are you in your workplace? Did you recently receive a promotion? Did you get fired? Did God move you to another church or neighborhood? Has He relocated you overseas?

Are you excelling as a leader in your environment? I don't just mean excelling as a Christian. I'm talking about being the best. I'm talking about taking the wisdom of Christ and throwing it at the foolishness of this world.

Are you the king's advisor, as Daniel was?

Daniel, although he found himself in the courts of a foreign king, could be an advisor to that king. Are you an advisor to the king? Are you an advisor to the systems of this world?

Is the world coming to you because you know more, work harder, look better, and you hold yourself up to a higher standard than anyone else? If you've been given a promotion, are you earning that promotion above and beyond?

Even Paul says, "If you're a slave to a master who is ungodly, you should serve him as unto the Lord. Excel as a slave!" Why did he say that? (Colossians 3:22-23)

He said it so that our light may shine. Our light shining means a lot more than being morally sound.

Being a Christian is a lot more than being nice to people. Thank the Lord for that!

*BEING A CHRISTIAN IS A LOT MORE THAN JUST OBEYING THE RULES. IT'S ABOUT MAKING THE RULES.*

Being an apostle in this movement goes far beyond looking like a good Christian in these environments. It's about making the rules. It's about being the model, the mentor, the leader, the most qualified, and the most capable.

# BECOME A TARE

> **Luke 6:45** *A good man out of the good treasure of his heart brings forth good; and an evil man out of the evil treasure of his heart brings forth evil. For out of the abundance of the heart his mouth speaks.*

Apostles, when share our knowledge and experience, even in worldly things, it comes from our spirits. Just like this scripture beautifully says, we release what is in our spirits through our words.

So, consider this. If believers are doing the educating, the leading, and the instructing, then we'll be the ones doing the influencing. The Spirit of Christ that's in us will be influencing the world.

I'm reminded of the parable where the servants came to the master and said, "Master, someone sowed tares among the wheat." It spoke about the sons of the enemy and about how the Lord would bring about a separation at the end of time (Matthew 13:24-60).

When I look at this parable, I think that I surely wouldn't mind changing things up and being a tare in the enemy's field. I would love to sneak into the enemy's camp, sow some weeds and mess up his crop for a change. I'm tired of it being the other way around.

Every believer is a seed in God's hand with the potential of power that this world has never seen. It's time that these seeds are sown\ into the soil of the world. I can't wait to see them popping up all over the place in the enemy's field.

> *EVERY SINGLE BELIEVER IS A SEED IN GOD'S HAND WITH THE POTENTIAL OF POWER THAT THIS WORLD HAS NEVER SEEN.*

We should see it in the field of the arts, psychology, finances, entertainment, and the medical systems. I would like to see a couple of Christian tares spreading their seeds in the business and commercial world. If we grasp the fullness of this movement, we will see Christians spearheading inventions and medical breakthroughs!

I would like to see these trees popping up everywhere and the rest of the world looking around thinking, "That's some really nice fruit. Can I have some of it?" We would become pillars in the world.

That is how we'll usher in this new move. The move won't be fed by one or two but by the Church as a collective.

Perhaps you're saying, "God, change me and bring me into the land that you've promised me! God, this doesn't look like what I asked you for. Why did you move me into the desert?"

God says, "I've moved you. I moved you to the desert. Water will flow from the rock."

> *WAKE UP! YOUR LAND DIDN'T LOOK LIKE WHAT YOU THOUGHT IT SHOULD LOOK LIKE, BUT WITH A LITTLE BIT OF WORK AND PRAYER THAT LAND CAN TRANSFORM INTO ONE THAT WILL FLOW WITH MILK AND HONEY.*

Your land didn't look like what you thought it would. However, with some apostolic grace and prayer it can be transformed into one that flows with milk and honey.

The Lord gave me a word for you. He said, "I've started a series of events in your life. You won't understand them. Some of the first steps that I lead you to take will be in the wilderness.

You'll go into the deep where you're surrounded by storms. Don't fight my hand, because those storms will move you to the place I need you positioned.

I will put your feet on a soil that you never knew existed.

I will bring forth a promise that you couldn't anticipate."

## THE PAJAMA APOSTLE

I hope that I've challenged the ministry=podium mentality. When I stand at the podium, it's such a small fraction of what I do for the Lord.

That platform will come and go. What I preach behind the pulpit today will be old hat next week. However, what I impart into the lives of my spiritual children remains. It's the hours I spend ministering in the kitchen, or in counseling rooms until late into the night that will remain to the next generation.

I've ministered most powerfully in my pajamas. It happened because we lived in ministry centers and had people in our home. The work that I do in my pajamas will remain.

This is where God put me. He established me as a mother to His people, and I will be the best mother that I can. I will parent the best way that I can. I will be a mother to mothers and an example to my sons.

I will shine in this place that He has given me because that's my place. I'm the Church, and the Church should be wherever you are.

# 8

# IDENTIFY THE SEASON OF MANDATE COMPLETION

***Isaiah 43:19*** *Behold, I will do a new thing, Now it shall spring forth; Shall you not know it? I will even make a road in the wilderness And rivers in the desert.*

I was pregnant with my youngest daughter and the year was 2001. As an over-confident prophet, I was training prophets into office.

I had no clue what I was doing or where I was going. I wonder what would happen if my "apostolic self" of today traveled to the moment my apostolic ministry was born?

It was during this time that the Lord shared the principles of the Davidic mandate with me. I was fearless, sharp, naïve, and ambitious. There is no way that the passionate newly appointed apostle would understand the "me" of today. I don't speak the same. I don't walk the same, and I don't think the same.

Through the process of my call, I've changed as God wanted me to change. Back then, I didn't have the eyes to see, or the ears to hear what God had planned. Yet, no matter how much we know we haven't arrived, we still cling to the slight understanding we have and make it out to be the whole.

Apostle, if you want to move forward in this new generation of the apostolic move, then there are some realities you need to face. The first is that your eyes have yet to see the part that God wants you to play!

You are clinging to such a small fragment of the vision that you cannot grasp its fullness.

## A Fragmented Vision

If you want to begin walking in the "today" vision that God has for you, it means realizing that you need a completely new perspective. And so, as the Lord reveals the fullness of your part to play, He will call you to seasons of blindness. Stick with me because I'm about to help you transition from one mandate to another.

*AS THE LORD REVEALS THE FULLNESS OF YOUR PART TO PLAY, HE WILL CALL YOU TO SEASONS OF BLINDNESS.*

The reason why you go through seasons of feeling blind is because God needs you to gain a new perspective. Wow... how hard do we fight God on this one? As apostles we are called to see for others. We're called to create patterns and lay out the structure. So, when God chooses to blind us for a season, it's crushing!

An apostle without vision is like a prophet without words to speak! I've done a lot of teaching on death of a vision. To clarify, that's not what I'm talking about here. I'm talking about what happens when the Lord needs you to transition.

I shared in *The Apostolic Mandate* that the Lord will give you an assignment to fulfill. When you complete that mandate, don't think that your job is done! Rather it's time to move on. Much like I had to through the years. I didn't stay a "trainer of trainers" forever. I didn't even stay as a prophetic apostle forever. As the needs of God's people changed, so did my anointing, gifts, and especially... my mandate.

## How Mandates Come to an End

So, let's step back a bit and look at what happens when you complete a mandate and what exactly that looks like.

## 1. Mandate Is Completed – Establishing a Monument

You might be like Solomon who completed his mandate to build the Temple. The worst mistake that I've seen many apostles make was to try and stick around to keep working land that had been fully utilized.

If you don't recognize when the mandate is fulfilled and you keep pushing forward with it, you'll begin to undo what you birthed in the first place. How many leaders have we seen make this mistake? They will reach the zenith of their mandate, raise up teams and establish their organization. However, they don't recognize the signs of the times.

They don't see nor sense the changes in the weather and when the Lord tries to take the ministry that He raised, they snatch it back and keep trying to "work it" using the tools that they did at the beginning.

Same old revival stories... much like the Israelite generation that told grand tales of the Red Sea parting and the mountains shaking. Today's generation is tired of the grand old tales and crave the reality of the Church today. The stories of yesterday won't establish a Church foundation for tomorrow.

*THE STORIES OF YESTERDAY WON'T ESTABLISH A CHURCH FOUNDATION FOR TOMORROW.*

When you refuse to step back and allow your old mandate to rest where it lies, you'll tear down what you built up. That mandate was built for a specific generation and time. Time to let go, Apostle.

Don't you admire monuments?

> ***Joshua 4:5*** *and Joshua said to them: "Cross over before the ark of the LORD your God into the midst of the Jordan, and each one of you take up a stone on his shoulder, according to the number of the tribes of the children of Israel,*
> *6 that this may be a sign among you when your children ask in time to come, saying, 'What do these stones mean to you?'*
> *7 Then you shall answer them that the waters of the Jordan were cut off before the ark of the covenant of the LORD; when it crossed over the Jordan, the waters of the Jordan were cut off. And these stones shall be for a memorial to the children of Israel forever."*

Joshua built such a monument to celebrate the completion of one mandate and the birth of another. Moses had completed his mandate by bringing God's people to the edge of the Promised

Land. Joshua's mandate was just about to begin as they prepared to take the land.

Your mandate, Apostle, broke ground. It brought you and God's people to the place where they're now. So, set up a monument! Hand the work over! Establish it to run itself! Then get up and get moving across the Jordan! It's time for you to shift and if you never allow your mandate to become that monument, you won't keep up with the next phase in God's building plan.

## 2. Mandate Cannot Be Completed

The Lord promised Abraham the land on which he walked, yet never possessed it. The most he could hold claim to, was a burial plot that he could lay beside his wife in.

Abraham was called to fulfill a purpose that would echo through generations, but he never got to see the completion thereof but he was also never meant to. His mandate was meant to "sit" until the people were ready. He entered into a covenant with the Lord. He prepared his son to take on the mantle. He blessed and prepared the way, but never got to fully establish it.

The children of Israel needed time to become a nation. They needed to go to Egypt for a couple of hundred years. So, they left the land of their father, Abraham, and joined Joseph in a very long season of transition.

Isn't it fascinating that one of the first places that they traveled to on the way to the Promised Land was to that burial plot to lay Joseph's bones to rest? A full circle had taken place. Abraham never got to see the mandate fulfilled and there are times when the Lord will have you, as an apostle, lay a foundation and start a movement, only to walk away.

Did you fail? No, the mandate is not ready to be fulfilled and you're just one person in the Lord's intricate plan. Had Abraham not taken time to birth the son he did, we wouldn't have the inheritance we do today! What a great boast. Abraham's grand accomplishment could be penned with but four words: "Abraham had a son".

Looking with natural eyes this doesn't look like a great man who changed the world. But wow, what a shockwave he released on this world with the birth of that one son. Thousands of years later and that covenant echoed once again when angels called on the shepherds in the field, as Jesus let out His first cry. What started with humble beginnings will have a greater impact than you realize, Apostle.

It's not just about the patterns you establish, but rather the one who imparted them to you. Not only does He have ownership of those patterns, but He is also well able to carry them to the next generation on His own terms.

So, recognize the signs! The doors close. The time goes by and you find yourself walking on a plateau that has no end. You keep looking back at the word God gave you. You keep trying to knock on the old doors. You try to flow in the old gifts and anointing but the power is no longer there.

It's time to walk away. It's time to let that mandate go and to allow the Lord to pick it up again when He deems fit to do so. Don't be surprised though, that when He does that you won't be the one He chooses to complete that mandate. Walk away! Allow the Holy Spirit to lead you into the shadow of the valley of death where you can neither see nor understand! It's here where you'll find your new vision waiting.

You won't find it in the dormant mandate in your hands. You won't find it looking back. You will find it by walking through the valley until you come out on the other side.

## 3. You Pass the Mandate On

I would dare say that it burns in us all to complete a mandate and then to be able to pass it on to others! Although a beautiful ideal, it's not as easy as you think. The reason why your mandate can be handed to another, is because you allowed it to evolve!

God's will and righteousness never change, but generations sure do. The way we talk, see life, and express ourselves, changes all the time. As nations we evolve and you can be sure that although God's plan is set in stone, the way it's expressed changes from generation to generation. When you allow the Lord to keep evolving you for each generation, then you'll be able to pass your mandate on to another.

When this happens, you need to realize that it's time for you to go to the top of your mountain and to die! How unfair was it for Moses to never set foot in that Promised Land? Well, that's what I always thought. That was until the Lord brought me through this transition. The transition of completing and handing my mandate over.

He said to me, "My child, do you think I was punishing Moses for not allowing him to lead my people into the Promised Land? No! Moses was 80 years old when he began leading my people. He survived attacks from the enemy, warfare within and without. He climbed the mountain many times and spent many hours judging my people.

He trained up Joshua and set the Tabernacle in place. The truth is that Moses was tired, and it was time for Joshua to pick up his sword in a capacity that Moses no longer could. I called Moses to that mountain top to rest. It was time for him to let go, knowing he had completed what I had asked of him!"

Check this out:

> **Exodus 3:9** *Now therefore, behold, the cry of the children of Israel has come to Me, and I've also seen the oppression with which the Egyptians oppress them.* **10** *Come now, therefore, and I will send you to Pharaoh that you may bring My people, the children of Israel, out of Egypt."*

Where in this passage does the Lord tell Moses that he was called to possess the Promised Land? God told Moses that he would lead his people out of Egypt. He more than fulfilled his mandate and yet also allowed it to evolve to the point where he could hand it on to Joshua.

Joshua had a perspective and grace Moses didn't. He was connected to the new generation as Moses wasn't. It was time for Moses to move on and Apostle, once you hand the work over, it's time for you to move on as well.

The reason being that to receive the new mandate that the Lord has for you, you need a new perspective. If you don't climb the mountain and turn your face towards the new horizon that God has for you, your vision will always be filled with your accomplishments of the past. You will never have the capacity to see into the future that God has planned.

## The Transition Between Mandates – Your Damascus Road Experience

When one mandate comes to an end and another begins, I liken it to Apostle Paul's Damascus road experience. He was on one assignment and with a sudden move of God's hand, he was on another.

We see Paul's passionate expression of his faith both before and after his conversion. Let's linger a while on that road with Paul as he encounters the Lord personally. We often liken our Christian experience to "seeing the light" and indeed that's exactly what Paul saw. However, instead of seeing further, he was blinded.

Scales formed on his eyes to the point where he needed be taken by the hand. How crushing it is for an apostle to lose vision! It feels like a punishment! For three very long days Paul had nothing to go on except what he felt in his newly born spirit. He had no human understanding to count on. He couldn't even navigate the house on his own!

All around him, circumstances were beginning to shift. As he lay blind in that room, the Holy Spirit was visiting Ananias and telling him to visit Paul. In that moment, the Lord lined up Paul's new mandate. By the time his vision returned he was ready to walk on a new path.

For us to truly see, sometimes we need to be blind for a while. We need to take our eyes off our agenda and understanding and allow the Lord time to give us a new perspective. If the Lord has called you as an apostle for today's generation, then don't become frustrated when your sight is taken from you.

> *FOR US TO TRULY SEE, SOMETIMES WE NEED TO BE BLIND FOR A WHILE.*

> ***1 Corinthians 2:9*** *But as it's written: "Eye has not seen, nor ear heard, nor have entered into the heart of man the things which God has prepared for those who love Him."*
> ***10*** *But God has revealed them to us through His Spirit. For the Spirit searches all things, yes, the deep things of God.*
> ***11*** *For what man knows the things of a man except the spirit of the man which is in him? Even so no one knows the things of God except the Spirit of God.*
> ***12*** *Now we have received, not the spirit of the world, but the Spirit who is from God, that we might know the things that have been freely given to us by God.*
> ***13*** *These things we also speak, not in words which man's wisdom teaches but which the Holy Spirit teaches, comparing spiritual things with spiritual.*
> ***14*** *But the natural man doesn't receive the things of the Spirit of God, for they're foolishness to him; nor can he know them, because they're spiritually discerned.*

Ears have not heard, nor eyes seen what God wants to do. So, wait a while and allow the Lord to paint the picture for you! Paul had no idea that his mandate would be to lay out church structure. The Lord had a lot of rearranging to do to make sure that Paul got the message.

## EMPTIED FOR PURPOSE

You're spiritually blinded by your mandate at this point. In many ways it shaped you as a person. The message you taught and the people you trained, shaped you. Your journey led you to this point and your mind, emotions, and will are all formed to accommodate that mandate.

Before you can move on to the new one that awaits, you need to be blinded for a little while. You need a hard drive reboot. I don't think we realize just how much we think, do, and push forward every single day. You only realize it when you're suddenly forced to sit down in the dark and wait.

God will not speak to you. You are shut down from everything that's familiar and all you can do... is wait! The year 2020 saw many apostles in this position and it gives me perspective on the fruit I see at present. While many mock the sudden rise of numerous apostles, I recognize the moment they were born – right there in the darkness of isolation.

> THE YEAR 2020 SAW MANY APOSTLES IN THIS POSITION AND IT GIVES ME PERSPECTIVE ON THE FRUIT I SEE AT PRESENT.

What kind of fruit will the generations, years from now, eat because of the transitions we face today? So, don't rush it. God has not been taken by surprise by your circumstance. Quite the contrary is true. He's the one who pummeled you with that great light. That moment of flash blindness has left you wondering what on earth just happened.

Rest, Apostle! Wait a while! Step back and allow the Lord to transition you, His way! The most frustrating part of this transition is that there is just nothing you can do about it. Paul had to just wait until Ananias came along to pray for him. He could not take the scales from his own eyes. He had to hear his mandate from Ananias. Talk about having to be dependent on someone else!

> **Acts 9:15** *But the Lord said to him, "Go, for he is a chosen vessel of Mine to bear My name before Gentiles, kings, and the children of Israel. For I will show him how many things he must suffer for My name's sake."*

We're accustomed to others leaning on us for direction. Yet, in this moment of transition, you'll indeed need others in your life to give you a new perspective.

## NEW PERSPECTIVE ON THE HORIZON

So, along with being blind, the Lord will lead other people into your life who don't see the same way you do. They will come from diverse life and doctrinal experiences. They will come with a message that doesn't sound clear to you. They will challenge character traits and perspectives in you that were never challenged before.

## IDENTIFY THE SEASON OF MANDATE COMPLETION

In many ways, you'll feel like that newly appointed apostle I described at the beginning. Naïve once again. Empty once again.

Although this might sound a bit dramatic, realize that along with the darkness comes a deep peace of being able to let go. I wonder how it must have felt for Moses on the top of that mountain as he overlooked the land one last time. Did he feel the burdens of the people roll off his shoulders? Did he breathe a sigh of relief knowing that he no longer had to fight for his convictions and protect those in his care?

Or did he feel the deep death? Did he weep as he looked over Canaan remembering the years of intercession and decree he endured to keep them moving? Was there a part of him that felt as if he failed?

I wonder because this is how I felt when the Lord took me through this season. Craig and I were in process of handing the Next Gen Prophets to Deborah-Anne and Michael for a year already. However in February 2025 at their first summit, it was a public announcement.

During worship I moved to the back of the hall, overlooking all of San Diego. The place I had spoken many decrees over. We had spent years pioneering. The Lord said to me, "Moses, it's time to die up on this mountain. It's time now to let go."

Legacy – it's everything I wanted. I just didn't expect a funeral service for the parts I'd never get to play.

It's a time of emptying. A time of laying it all down and recognizing that the Lord gives,

> IT'S A TIME OF EMPTYING. A TIME OF LAYING IT ALL DOWN AND RECOGNIZING THAT THE LORD GIVES, AND THE LORD TAKES AWAY.

and the Lord takes away. Your load is light, and your burden is made easy.

How long and hard have you run, Apostle? How empty do you feel today? You have received so many visions through the years. Many times, they felt like a weight on your shoulders. Some you fulfilled and others you didn't. There are those where you secretly hang your head in shame feeling like you let the Lord down.

It's okay to stop running now. It's okay to sit in the darkness for a while and to allow the Lord to give you vision once again. The darkness is not a punishment, it's an invitation to gain a new perspective. Vision is born in darkness and the sooner you let go of your striving, the sooner you'll be ready to see again. Let the old mandate die within you! Grieve and then allow another conception to take place!

The Lord knows how much time you need. He understands that it takes time for us to let go. It takes time for us to be willing to set our sights on something unfamiliar.

## The Apostolic Movement Is Upon Us

> **Dictionary definition of movement:** an act of changing physical location or position or of having things changed.
>
> **Synonyms:** Change, fluctuation, rise, fall, variation, trend

Where you stood yesterday is not where the Lord is calling you to stand today, or tomorrow, for that matter. One thing that's constant in this apostolic movement, is a continual evolution of who you are and what you're called to do.

So, you started off with a Davidic mandate and trained your mighty men? Has it occurred to you that God might be calling you as a Joseph to the marketplace now? Did you start off in the marketplace and now God is shutting it down and calling you to teach?

Change! Evolve! Move on! Be part of the plan for this generation and the one to come!

The mandates of the past remain as a monument of what we have established, but until we allow our vision to change, we become that monument in its place – stuck in the past.

Being part of God's movement comes with a price and if as apostles we are not prepared to allow God to change our perspectives, what hope does the rest of the Church have?

I'm down for it, how about you? Embrace your Damascus! Cling to Jesus in the darkness! Then, wait! The light is coming, Apostle, and with it, new vision.

# 9

# FROM TABERNACLE TO TEMPLE

***1 Chronicles 16:1** So they brought the ark of God, and set it in the midst of the tabernacle that David had erected for it. Then they offered burnt offerings and peace offerings before God.*

One of David's first acts as king was to bring back the ark. Only he didn't put it back into the Tent of Meeting. Rather, he established what was known as the Tabernacle of David. He brought the ark into the Tabernacle of David. He instituted 24-hour praise, worship and prophecy. Israel, as a nation under God, was about to undergo another massive shift in their identity.

We had these two structures, the Tent of Meeting and the Tabernacle of David. Sacrifices continued in the Tent of Meeting while praise and worship continued in the Tabernacle of David. The Tent of Meeting had a veil, but the Tabernacle of David didn't. God was already dismantling what was familiar to them.

Later you'll read how Solomon maintained organization, holy furnishings, and a pattern.

# Tent of Meeting

> *1 Kings 8:3 So all the elders of Israel came, and the priests took up the ark.*
> *4 Then they brought up the ark of the Lord, the tabernacle of meeting, and all the holy furnishings that were in the tabernacle. The priests and the Levites brought them up.*
> *5 Also King Solomon, and all the congregation of Israel who were assembled with him, were with him before the ark, sacrificing sheep and oxen that could not be counted or numbered for multitude.*
> *6 Then the priests brought in the ark of the covenant of the Lord to its place, into the inner sanctuary of the temple, to the Most Holy Place, under the wings of the cherubim.*

From this point onward the Scriptures don't reference the Tabernacle and Tent of Meeting. After this, we only learn of the Temple that Solomon built.

A tent is great for the wilderness. While you were a rolling stone, bumping here and there and trying to figure out your way, you needed a tent. You needed something that you could change and adapt at will.

Your apostolic structure needed to be fluid. You needed to think on your feet. Yet, a time is coming to build the temple. A new set of rules will apply. You cannot use your tent anymore.

Good news, you get to keep the furniture. Bad news, the tent has to go. We love the prophetic phrase, "God wants to increase your tent pegs."

*DUMP THE TENT! BUILD A TEMPLE! GOD WANTS YOU TO ESTABLISH SOMETHING IN THE LAND THAT WILL REMAIN.*

No, God wants to throw away your tent. Dump the tent! Build a temple! God wants you to establish something in the land that will remain. Yet, you cannot understand why the first gust of wind comes and blows your tent away.

"The devil is getting me now. Every time God tries to move, the devil tries to get me."

No, you're in a tent. If the wind blows, of course it's going to fall down. You're expecting something of your vision that will never happen. It's not built to last. A temple is built to last.

"Lord, can we have a temple and a tent? I'm really close to my tent. It cost a pretty penny!"

Do you know how many times Moses, had to climb that mountain to get the pattern for that tent?

That was a lot of climbing for an old man. When we were in Switzerland, I could barely handle walking up what they called a little hill. This is a man who paid the price for God, up and down and up and down. They didn't have trams in those days.

You've paid a price for your perfect, little tent. You've put flowers on it, and you've made it home. You're so comfortable with it, and you're trying to take it into the next season.

## THE RAIN IS COMING

I'm here to warn you that if you push it too far - that tent will fall flat on you. It's because it cannot withstand the wind and the rain that are coming. You cannot foresee the move of God that's coming, and how He will use you within that move.

However, you're so comfortable with your position, your tent, your accomplishments, your ministry, your team, your pattern, and your plan. If God told you to wipe the slate clean and dig a new foundation, you would say, "That cannot be the voice of God. I've spent the last 20 years establishing this tent."

Yet, it's still just a tent.

When Solomon dedicated that Temple to the Lord, the priests could not stand to minister under the glory. The "more" came when the Temple was in place. Are you prepared to pay the price for the "more"? You cannot go forward looking back!

If you want a new vision, a greater power and ability to do the work of God, then you need a new blueprint. This is especially difficult for any of us who are called to the apostolic.

Do you know what defines the apostle from any of the other fivefold ministry leaders?

## APOSTOLIC EVOLUTION

It's that he is one who is prepared to evolve. He is one who is prepared to go up the mountain, get the pattern, and start all over with another pattern, for every single season. He never stays with one pattern or mandate, in one place.

"I've got my mandate."

Hooray for you. The next apostle is already onto number five. Do you know why?

It's because the people of God change, and society changes. God is on a timetable. Are you going to walk according to God's timetable, or are you going to fossilize?

"I'm happy with my little church."

Yes, you and a million other status quo pastors. You have so much to say about leaders who are stuck in the past, but then God says to you, "Come, give me that tent of meeting ..."

"But Lord, that's all I have."

"It's okay. That is all I need."

Let's build. Once Solomon had established the Temple, he established something in the land that would remain. Further down the road the children of Israel failed God so badly, they were exiled. However, when they repented and God began restoration of their land to them, what was the first thing He did?

He sent Ezra and Nehemiah to build the Temple and the walls that surrounded the city. They built something that would remain.

What kind of ministry do you really want? What is your fire?

Is it to have a tent that can be blown away by the wind tomorrow?

## WHAT WILL YOU PASS ON?

When I die one day, I don't want to hand my sons and daughters a tent.

That is like giving them a pair of worn-out shoes or my

> WHEN I DIE ONE DAY, I DON'T WANT TO HAND MY SONS AND DAUGHTERS A TENT.

original wedding dress. It's sweet and all but looking back I'm not even sure I would wear the same wedding dress given another chance. Times have changed! Fashions have changed! Should I be insulted because my daughters would not want my raggedy old wedding dress? Then why should I give them a raggedy old ministry tent?

However, it's much different if we build a temple and establish a pattern that has a foundation that goes deep into the ground and cannot be moved. I want you to see that picture in your mind.

We're so foolish. We think, "This is it. This is my ministry, my call, and my vision."

We hang on as if this is the only one God has up His sleeve. You are so afraid to take the risk and give it all to Him, and just wipe it all to start afresh with a whole new concept.

"Was it because I failed, I was wrong, or I didn't hear God?"

No, God is just done with that season.

"But it's all I know how to do."

Then you better learn something else.

Do you still think that God's the one holding you back, or are you perhaps limiting the hand of God?

God is trying to evolve you so that you might establish something new. If you insist on holding onto your tent of meeting, you'll stay in the wilderness.

Are you eating the fruit of your promise yet? Are you at the place in your call right now where you can say, "This is it! Everywhere I place my feet, this is the land He has given me"?

If not, then it's time to start building. You cannot work this up. You can only work up so much in the wilderness. The vision that God gave you and the work that you've accomplished isn't about good, bad, failure, or success. It's about the process.

We're so finite in our thinking.

"I must do this to impress the Lord. I must do this to serve the Lord. I must fulfill the call to make God happy with me."

All the while, God is sending you in many directions to get through to you, to change you, to establish you, to answer the cries of His people. His plan is to establish His pattern in the earth. The sad truth is that we all think it depends on us.

Aren't we just a little bit arrogant?

"My ministry is the ministry that's going to change the world. I cannot let this ministry go. If I let this ministry go, I let everything go. I let God go, and I let His people go."

Seriously, just you?

How many other apostles does He have, just in your region?

# Dare You Step Out and Fly?

Dare you step out into air and fly? Dare you jump and see if He catches you? Even if He doesn't, then maybe you just need to be dead for a while until He is ready to resurrect you! I want you to break free a little. We tie ourselves up so much with do's, don'ts, and what-ifs.

You are so afraid to miss that one tiny visitation from God that He might give you. You think this is the one door for you to walk through and establish your ministry. As if God is so limited and all He has is one tiny little door for you.

God is infinite. If you miss this door, He has another one.

"I missed my time of visitation. I'm never going to rise up and be the prophet, apostle, or leader that He has called me to be."

This mindset isn't scriptural. Gabriel came to where Mary was. When Samson's mother had her angelic visitation, she had the angel sit around long enough to get her husband, so that the angel could tell him the news also. God is patient and He is not going to drop-kick a visitation when you're not looking and then make a run for it! (Judges 13)

We think like this because we so desperately want to please Him and be in His will. We want to experience His blessing, and we want to know that whatever we are doing in this earth, it's to establish His Kingdom.

We think that if we step to the left or right or fail, that we aren't going to establish His Kingdom. As if it was done by our might and our power.

Perhaps God just really needed you to mess up, in order to establish His Kingdom.

## The Tabernacle of David

Look at Moses and David. They made mistakes and it was just what God needed, at the right time. Break free of your ministry and your tent. Cut the tent pegs and roll it up but keep the furnishings.

There are elements that you've lived that are precious. Your journey was never about the tent. It was about the Ark within it.

It was the furnishings within that counted. That's why you went through the process that created the apostle that stands tall today. The tent was just there to give them a roof over their heads. The real business went on inside of it.

We have our little structure and pattern, how we preach and teach, what our principles are, and the kind of people we want to reach.

"I have a women's ministry. I have a children's ministry. I have a ministry to my region."

These are all just tents!

"I'm called to the Jews. I'm called to the Gentiles." Peter did a lot more with the Jewish church and Paul with the Gentile church than lead them to salvation. No, Apostle, they began a movement together. They left behind a trail of doctrine, laws, and precepts we now apply to our temple!

Put that fire of yours in a temple, and let's see what happens. When they brought the Ark into the Temple, the glory of God came down. The promise of God came to pass.

The Lord said, "Whoever comes to worship here, I will hear His prayer, and I will answer." (1 Kings 9:3)

Indeed, He did that and made Solomon one of the most successful kings in Jewish history. You see your promise, and you see God leading you in this direction. Yet, we get too fixated on what we have done, and what we have built.

It's not bad, guys. What you've done for God up until now was good. You've been in His will. This took me a long time to understand.

God started to shift me, and I said, "Lord, did I fail that you keep moving me out of my place?

He said, "No, the job was done. When that which is perfect has come, that which is in part shall be done away. It came, it was perfect, and it was done. Get the memo and move on."

"But Lord, I don't feel like I really dug in there."

*HOW CAN THE LORD BRING A MOVEMENT TO PASS, IF YOU'RE NOT PREPARED TO MOVE?*

This has to be about what He wants, and what He wants is a movement. How can the Lord bring a movement to pass, if you're not prepared to move?

## Season to Season

It's not comfortable because He doesn't call us to do what we are capable of doing. How else could His glory be displayed through us, unless we are foolish?

It's time to be foolish again.

"What are you doing? You have built up this whole work, and you're just going to start over? Why would you do that? Why would you give up something that's established?"

Because God said so!

After the Temple was constructed, we don't read about the Tabernacle anymore. However, you do read about the glory of the Temple.

Here you're with your worn-out tent that's breezy at night and hot in the day. The critters come up from underneath this little tent, and you're always having to patch and fix it.

In your future, God has a temple covered in gold and glory for you.

I see so many stick to that moth-eaten tent, and they work it and work it. They're still telling the same stories and preaching on the same revelations and principles. Everybody is bored. It's time to move on. You have beaten that message to death. It's time for a new revelation. It's time to build the temple.

# 10

# MAKING THE TEMPLE TRANSITION

When God transitions us to build, the first step is to lay down what would hinder the process. The price is different for each of us, depending on mandate. However, here are some pointers to help you make that transition.

## 1. WHAT IS THE ONE THING YOU DO NOT WANT TO GIVE UP?

What price aren't you willing to pay? What is the one thing that you don't want to give up?

It could be something physical, or it could be a ministry.

Abraham was asked to sacrifice Isaac. Moses had to give up his place of hiding. Paul had to give up his position of merit as a Pharisee. Israel had to give up their false gods. What do you withhold from God?

The old weighs down your vision for the future. And usually it's bound up in the one thing we refuse to give up.

For me, it was my family and ministry team. How nonsensical! Why would God ask me to surrender the one thing that took most of my apostolic process to develop.

Because, in the pursuit of team building I lost sight of the bigger picture. You become comfortable in what works. You hide behind it. It becomes your identity.

And so the shaking begins. Not for harm, but for evolution. I couldn't embrace the fullness of my apostolic identity while I hid behind those I equipped. The Lord had a bigger task for Craig and I and it went beyond team building. He was calling us, once again to the nations... and not everyone was invited this time.

So I get Abraham. We see the aspects of covenant in God's request for Isaac's sacrifice. However, I wonder how much of Abraham's identity was now found in his son.

God called Abraham to so much more. His covenant with God would be in the establishment of a natural Kingdom in the form of Israel. However, it would also be in the establishment of a spiritual one!

When Abraham followed through, his greater purpose was set in stone. On that day he became the father of those natural seeds, as the grains of sand. He also became the spiritual father of those spiritual seeds, as stars of the sky!

## 2. What Feels Like It has Died?

Yes, the tent housed the glory of God. Inscribe its story on a monument and pick up a trowel. The seasons have changed and winter has set in on the old. The anointing doesn't flow like it used to. The numbers have declined. You struggle to push out another sermon or revelation.

The fast flowing river has become stifled to a trickle and you feel abandoned by God. Nope, the Brook Cherith dried up because you're called to higher things.

It's harder every day to stir up everyone's fire for the vision. In fact, you spend more time putting out fires than pioneering in new territory.

These aren't signs of failure. They're signs that evolution is underway. In the same way a caterpillar winds itself into a chrysalis, your ministry is enduring change.

Did you know that the caterpillar isn't built for long-term survival? Without metamorphosis it can't develop wings, reproductive organs, or an adult body. It would fail to reach adulthood and endure an untimely death. Dark... I know.

Yet a fitting illustration for my point. What might feel like death, is a call to evolution. The blindness stage is the most daunting of all. There's nothing to be done inside the chrysalis but to wait.

And so we're reminded that we never submitted a CV for this call. We were picked out from our mother's womb.

## APOSTOLIC TRENDSETTERS

> **Daniel 2:21** *And He changes the times and the seasons; He removes kings and raises up kings; He gives wisdom to the wise And knowledge to those who have understanding.*

We need to establish the Church for generations to come, and that means doing it in a way it has not been done before.

You cannot go forward while looking back.

Those old revivals are just that, old revivals. We don't want any more old revivals.

> YOU CANNOT GO FORWARD WHILE LOOKING BACK.

We want a reformation. We want something that will remain from generation to generation.

We don't want a big tent revival.

We want to establish the kingdom and build a temple in the earth.

We're bringing reformation to every community, and it's here to stay. It's not going to come for one or two little meetings and then go home and pack up, leaving everybody to be attacked by the devil the rest of the week.

> **Psalm 1:3** *He shall be like a tree Planted by the rivers of water, That brings forth its fruit in its season, Whose leaf also shall not wither; And whatever he does shall prosper.*

No! God wants us to begin laying down roots that dig deep into the soil and bear fruit from generation to generation. This is fruit that comes in its season. It's a tree whose leaves don't wither so that God might be glorified.

It comes at a cost. However, I tell you this, through every generation, Genesis to Revelation, it took only one person to turn the tide.

## Changing the Tide

There was always someone who was prepared to let go of their "sure thing" to walk on water. If you want your safety net, then God will give one to you.

However, you'll never walk on water or say to the winds and waves, "Peace, be still." It takes trendsetters and trailblazers to start a movement. Those with a fire to take the risk and trust God at His word.

> IT TAKES TRENDSETTERS AND TRAILBLAZERS TO START A MOVEMENT. THOSE WITH A FIRE TO TAKE THE RISK AND TRUST GOD AT HIS WORD.

They step out on the water, even though the winds and waves are blowing, knowing they risk their very lives. They step out into the unknown, and God meets them at their point of faith.

When a man or a woman of God steps out like that, they change the course of nations. Study church history. See the price our matriarchs and patriarchs paid.

## A New Pattern

Are you a living sacrifice, given up as an acceptable gift to God?

Only our surrender is acceptable to Him, not perfection. He doesn't need our perfection. He just needs our surrender.

> *ONLY OUR SURRENDER IS ACCEPTABLE TO HIM, NOT PERFECTION. HE DOESN'T NEED OUR PERFECTION. HE JUST NEEDS OUR SURRENDER.*

God might not want to actually take those things from you, but are you prepared to put them on the altar?

It's so easy to say, "Yes, of course. If God asks me, then I will."

Alright, God is asking you. What are you going to do?

"If He would ask me, I know that I would give it up."

Good. Let's go there.

What plans would you make today to give it up? What changes would you make right now in your circumstances to walk away, to go into the unknown, to be like Abraham, and to walk it out?

## ABRAHAM... LET'S TAKE A HIKE!

"I will send you on a journey and wherever you put your feet, I will give that land to you and your descendants. However, by the way, you won't ever own any of the land. You will just walk on it.

Also, you'll have a son who will have sons, and they'll be slaves for a couple hundred years before they come back. So, you won't even see the land, Abraham. You won't smell or taste it. All you'll get is a gravesite."

## MAKING THE TEMPLE TRANSITION

> *THAT IS THE ONLY LAND THAT ABRAHAM POSSESSED WHEN HE DIED - A TOMB! WELCOME TO APOSTOLIC MINISTRY.*

That is the only land that Abraham possessed when he died - a tomb. Welcome to apostolic ministry. That is all the land that we get to possess as well - the perpetual call to death. That is what remains constant.

When you come to that place, God can do incredible things through you.

How many more times must God repeat Himself through your journals, prophets, and circumstances? Do you want to possess your promised land?

You can be like Abraham and walk on it, or you could be like Solomon and establish a kingdom.

You can buy a plot of land, and it will be beautiful. However, only when you cultivate it, build on it, and sink your hands into the soil, will you possess it.

It's time to pull up the tent pegs and let the tent fall. By all means, gather the holy furnishings and bring the Ark with you. Cling to the anointing, fire, power, ability, and passion.

Then, begin construction!

## BURN THE PROMISES

Remember when I shared about the list of promises God asked me to burn?

I said, "Lord, how do I know what is of you and what is not of you? What must I give up and what not?"

He said, "Just put it all on the fire, Colette. If I find gold, it will be purified. If I find dross, it will be burned up."

All the holy furnishings were made of gold. Those things inside of you that He has spent so many years establishing are made of gold. Never be afraid to give it all up and put it all on the altar, because that which is gold will indeed remain.

Yet, make no mistake… the tent will burn.

## Make the Transition Already!

When you realize that the wall you're facing is not one of failure, but of promise, it changes your perspective. For how long has the Lord promised you a greater vision than you anticipated? Could David have imagined the grandeur of the Temple? His experience took him only so far.

Of all the courts of kings both domestic and abroad, could David have imagined a grander throne room and temple in all the world? It took a king who wasn't scorched by war… a child. One who was naïve enough to step out and use his wisdom without fear or reservation.

And so, the Lord calls you back to that naïveté of your spiritual childhood, back to the passionate apostle who went where angels feared to tread! You are well able to embrace a new mandate. Allow the Lord to shift your perspective! Stop grieving over the tent of the past.

Then, set your eyes forward and your steps of wisdom will be apparent. You will establish a mandate for generations to follow.

# MAKING THE TEMPLE TRANSITION

# 11

# THE THREE REALMS THAT DENOTE APOSTOLIC MATURITY

*2 Timothy 3:16* *All Scripture is given by inspiration of God, and is profitable for doctrine, for reproof, for correction, for instruction in righteousness,*
*17 that the man of God may be complete, thoroughly equipped for every good work.*

We've misunderstood the concept of ministry maturity in our dispensation. We gauge it by the size of a congregation or the number of miracles in a service. Step back and read that passage again. The word "work" mentioned here is the Greek word ergō meaning to toil or labor. It also refers to business and employment.

In other words, the Lord requires you to be equipped in any and every good deed you put your hand to. This goes way beyond ministry.

Does a flourishing ministry denote the success laid out for us in 2 Tim 3:16? When I see an apostle, with a thriving ministry but is three times divorced, I have questions. He harangues people for money because he has no financial savvy and doesn't understand the concept of moderation. Regardless of how huge his congregation is, I don't see a man who's fully equipped for every good work!

He's seriously immature in a couple of areas of his life. So yes, building your temple will solidify you in your mandate, but that's not the entirety of who you are. Your temple is not the fullness of your identity as an apostle.

*YOUR TEMPLE IS NOT THE FULLNESS OF YOUR IDENTITY AS AN APOSTLE.*

It's just one part of the whole. Solomon didn't stop at building the Temple. His mandate stretched out much further than that. He sent out ships of Tarshish for trade. For us to usher in this apostolic movement, we'll need a whole lot more than some good-looking temples.

*TO USHER IN THIS APOSTOLIC MOVEMENT, WE'LL NEED A WHOLE LOT MORE THAN SOME GOOD-LOOKING TEMPLES.*

We need some ships of Tarshish and a palace as well. When I share about becoming established, go back to the beginning of this book when I shared that to possess this land, we need to build on it. Let logic lead you here... how big do you think the Temple was? According to biblical measurements, it had a footprint of 3000 square feet.

Jerusalem in comparison was over 1 million square feet in size.

So yes, the Temple was central, and I will go on to share with you why it's vital you establish it first. However, it was only one small part of what established the Kingdom under Solomon.

The people of God need more from you. Only the Levites centered their lives around the Temple. The rest of God's people worked the fields and performed commerce in the city.

Those far from the Temple enjoyed a yearly pilgrimage! This is not enough to establish a kingdom. Perhaps your little kingdom, but certainly not the Kingdom of God. So, please can we move beyond our personal platforms again?!

Allow me to broaden your thinking and to challenge your limitation.

## THE THREE REALMS

> *1 Thessalonians 5:23 Now may the God of peace Himself sanctify you completely; and may your whole spirit, soul, and body be preserved blameless at the coming of our Lord Jesus Christ.*

Apostolic maturity comes by establishing all three realms of your influence in this world. Isn't it poetic how the number three is the Lord's number for perfection and completeness? Father, Son and Spirit create the Trinity. We're created, as human beings, in spirit, soul, and body. Then, we have the greatest influence in three realms on this earth.

*APOSTOLIC MATURITY COMES BY ESTABLISHING ALL THREE REALMS OF YOUR INFLUENCE IN THIS WORLD.*

These realms are:

1. The Ministry Realm: Your Temple
2. The Business Realm: Your Ships of Tarshish

3. The Social Realm: Your Palace

These three realms encompass all of our life and we are meant to walk in completeness, being fully equipped in all three of these areas.

I've lost count on how many anointed men and women of God were derailed by imbalances in one of these realms. So, if you think that putting everything you are into ministry is going to make you complete, you're in for a bumpy ride!

Do you know what this tells me if you're at church every day and never have time to take care of your family at home? It tells me that you're incomplete. Ministry is only one realm. Also, can we just move on with the pillar of fire here, guys? The "man for the hour" dynamic has long been dead and gone!

*THE "MAN FOR THE HOUR" DYNAMIC HAS LONG BEEN DEAD AND GONE!*

# WELCOME TO A NEW ERA

The picture of the sweet little "first lady" holding her crochet club for the ladies every Wednesday night, was buried in the sand of yesterday. Time to move on to the new Church era, Apostle! It's just not good enough anymore to coast on the anointing.

Solomon did a whole lot more than build a Temple and by the time you're through with the next couple of chapters, you'll see just how incredible this mandate is that God has given to you.

He shut you down on one realm, because He wants to build you up on the other two. So no, you're not missing God because you feel led to go into business. You are not missing God because you find yourself in the world networking with unbelievers.

However, let me backtrack a little here. Let's look at where we have been stuck as a Church for way too long.

## SOME CHURCH REALITIES THAT NEED TO CHANGE

The Church goes to the Lord for ministry. The Church goes to the world for business. As for our entertainment, relationships, and social interaction... Lord help us! Is it really necessary for me to point out some of the places that believers find themselves to meet these cravings within?

It's time that all three of these realms are brought to balance.

Until you bring them all into perspective, you'll remain imbalanced. Without maturity, it only takes a financial crisis to destroy your ministry. It takes just a spiritual crisis to destroy your business. Then, it will just take a relationship crisis to destroy both your ministry and business.

Until you're solid in these three realms, satan will always have something to trip you up with. I guarantee that you can pick out one of these three areas where you've fallen flat on your face repeatedly, and every time you fell, everything came tumbling down along with you.

You were incomplete. Apostolically immature. The reason why God would slow down your ministry and thrust you into the workplace is for the point of maturing you in all three realms.

## What's Wrong With People?

Receiving the anointing is the easy part. Learning to work with people... not so much. I don't know what is wrong with people. They just won't see things my way!

They won't do what I want them to do and they won't do it how I want them to do it! Yeah... I had a little bit of building to do in my social realm. I could engender a ton of respect while behind the pulpit but as things turned out, most of God's people weren't on the stage.

If I wanted to make a lasting change, it involved learning new perspectives and making new friends.

## Your Apostolic Blueprint

If there is ever one who really understood the power of these three realms, I would have to say it was King Solomon. (Although I think he overdeveloped the social realm just a tad... )

Now, we know his famous prayer for wisdom and the promises God made him. David instructed and trained Solomon so that he might build the Temple. Then came that day of dedication! Solomon asked the Lord to make the Temple His dwelling place and then... Well, if you don't read the first verse of the next chapter correctly, you might assume that God answered Solomon that night in a dream.

However, check this out... After all that, there is this passage:

> ***1 Kings 9:1*** *And it came to pass, when Solomon had finished building the house of the Lord and the king's*

> *house, and all Solomon's desire which he wanted to do,*
> *2 that the Lord appeared to Solomon the second time, as He had appeared to him at Gibeon.*
> *3 And the Lord said to him: "I've heard your prayer and your supplication that you've made before Me; I've consecrated this house which you've built to put My name there forever, and My eyes and My heart will be there perpetually.*

God appeared to Solomon the first time at Gibeon before the Temple was built. This was his moment to shine with the, "Give me wisdom" prayer.

So when we read about his second encounter, we assume it came directly after the temple dedication and "glory filled the temple" moment.

But it didn't. Solomon's second encounter and answer to his prayer came about 20 years into his reign.

## GET YOUR HOUSE IN ORDER, APOSTLE

God waited for Solomon to get his house in order before giving him that word.

How long have you waited for God to answer a prayer? Solomon prayed at the consecration of the Temple and then waited exactly 13 years before God answered. Not a whisper, until his palace was built.

The Lord used this passage to open my vision.

I've seen people passionately on fire for God. They dive headlong into ministry and then hit a roadblock. God says, "Get your house in order."

"Yes, but Lord... the call! Look at the temple I've consecrated. Answer my prayer, Lord."

However, God made Solomon wait and He will make you wait as well!

I really challenged you in the previous chapters to start building your temple and it's pretty self-explanatory that I'm speaking of your ministry. That is the "Glory! Hallelujah! More Lord. Bring down the fire!"

Indeed, the temple should be the first thing that you establish in your life. By giving the Lord license in your life by "Seeking first the Kingdom", you lay a foundation for the rest of the realms. The Lord comes first. The foundation of the temple must be laid.

## The Anointing Empowers You

It's when you've received God's anointing and wisdom that you're empowered to build the other two realms.

Solomon's second building project was his palace. That is the picture of your social realm. I will talk a little bit about that in a while. You see, Solomon didn't just go around building any old temple. He built it according to the pattern David had given to him.

He didn't just "wing it". He had a very clear picture of what He was commissioned to build. When I'm talking about building your ministry, I don't mean, "I'm called to prophesy, so I will go to churches and prophesy over everybody."

## Establishing Apostolic Structure

That is not what it takes to build a temple. Building the temple is not just having a praise and worship service. This is not the Tabernacle of David any longer, Apostle, this is the Temple now.

When I say, "build your temple", I mean to have a clear picture and pattern for ministry. Solomon was blessed because he got his pattern from the Lord through David.

> *1 Chronicles 28:19 All this," said David, "the LORD made me understand in writing, by His hand upon me, all the works of these plans."*

Tell me, what is your pattern for ministry?

"I'm called to be an apostle."

No, I didn't ask you what your gifts and calling are. I said, "What is your pattern for ministry?"

## Show Me Your Pattern in Writing

You see, even the Early Church had a pattern for ministry. The Scriptures tell us that they broke bread daily in fellowship and then continued in the doctrine of the apostles. There was a very clear pattern that was laid out in the Early Church.

You think, "I've established my ministry road and all is well."

Just because you flow in a couple of gifts and you have a couple of ministries under your belt, doesn't mean you've built a temple. No, what pattern do you have that others can use as a blueprint?

In the Early Church, the Apostles laid the doctrine. The elders took the doctrine and they built on it. They ran with it to the point where they could go and start churches on their own.

## The Early Church Pattern

We see early believers establish the church of Antioch overnight with their Gospel message. Consider this though. Not only did they spread the Gospel, but once people started getting saved, these new converts knew well enough to gather the people together and start a church!

Yes, they had the Holy Spirit who gave them the anointing and ability. However, you and I both know that it's one thing to have an anointing and another to know what to do with it. Yet these young believers knew what to do. Why? Well, they had been following the apostles' doctrine. They had a blueprint that could be duplicated time and again.

If you've ever been in ministry, you know that it's great to be in your prayer closet and to feel the presence of the Lord. However, it's another to know when to speak, when not to speak, what to speak, how to speak, and who to speak to. There is a pattern involved.

Guys, I know that I'm not the only apostle out there who comes across passionate believers who just received a revelation of their call saying, "I cannot wait to be in full-time ministry."

"Yes, and when you get there, what do you plan to do?"

"I will just go and minister to people. I will have a pulpit ministry."

It's like a farmer saying, "I cannot wait to be a farmer."

## THE THREE REALMS THAT DENOTE APOSTOLIC MATURITY

"What land do you have to farm?"

"I will take a bag of seeds and will just throw those seeds. I will head to my field and just throw, throw, throw."

One of my spiritual sons was a farmer who taught me what this process looks like. Up until I was educated, I figured that to farm meant having land, buying seed, sowing the seed, reaping the harvest, and then repeat.

I was such a greenhorn! Turns out that if I followed my pattern, I would be a very hungry farmer! No, to yield a good harvest, they have to plant a certain crop in its season because it deposits certain nutrients in the soil that the next (and different) crop will need.

*THE KINGDOM OF GOD HAS ALWAYS BEEN SET IN TIMESTAMPS AND PATTERNS.*

The Kingdom of God has always been set in timestamps and patterns. The reason why we are seeing so much chaos in the Church is because there is so much running around and people throwing their seeds everywhere.

Then, you wonder why the birds are eating it up. You are wondering why they're being choked by the weeds. It's because you're throwing them everywhere, instead of in the soil where they can produce a full harvest.

We need a structure in the body of Christ, but I'm not talking about the kind of structure that says, "We sing three hymns, we sing two songs, and then we have our prayer book." Can we break out of the mold, Apostle?

Did the year 2020 not teach us enough already? Yet still we want to stick to the way of doing things... just do it online now! We still want to play church and cling to our platforms when God has gone to such efforts to change things up. I already told you – dump that tent! It has so many limitations.

What is the worst thing that could happen if you decided to do church in a way no one ever saw it before? Well, it sounds to me then, that you would be building your own temple based on the pattern that God has given to you as an apostle!

# 12

# THE MINISTRY REALM: YOUR TEMPLE

> *1 Kings 6:1 And it came to pass in the four hundred and eightieth year after the children of Israel had come out of the land of Egypt, in the fourth year of Solomon's reign over Israel, in the month of Ziv, which is the second month, that he began to build the house of the Lord.*

This was a plan that was 480 years in the making. Look at the detail in just verse one. Solomon only began construction of the Temple after four years on the throne. Why a four-year delay?

David came up with the idea for a Temple. God gave him the blueprint by inspiration (1 Chron 22:6-10). However, it wasn't time to build.

He purchased Ornan's threshing floor as the Temple site. However, still it wasn't time to build. David raised the money and still God would not allow him to build. Then, Solomon became king, and you would think that the first thing that he would do on day 1, would be to begin building. Daddy gave him the pattern, he had the money, and everybody was behind him.

Yet, there were still a couple of things that Solomon had to do first. He had to be positioned. His kingdom had to be ready. Then, some people needed to be removed.

*GOD POSITIONED US YEARS AGO, IN PREPARATION FOR THE NEEDS OF THE CHURCH TODAY.*

God began this movement many years ago. He positioned you years ago, in preparation for the needs of the church today.

## REQUIREMENTS TO BUILD

Take some time to think about the circumstances that were required for Solomon to build that Temple. Firstly, the people had to be in a season of peace. What was the use of building a Temple that would just be torn down by war?

Also, the king was never home long enough to build it. So, what happened with the rule of David? David prepared the way with more than just a pattern and a trust fund. He did so much more. He took the land.

David spent most of his lifetime, conquering that Promised Land. He was taking the land that those in the time of Joshua didn't finish taking. He took the land and the people entered into rest. They entered a season of peace.

## TRANSITION FROM WAR TO PEACE IS A BATTLE!

Not so fast though. The writer of Hebrews tells us to "labor to enter into rest" (Heb. 4:11) Solomon lived this for real!

He killed Adonijah, Joab, and Shimei. Then he finished the job by banishing Abiathar the priest.

There's a slight transition between the dismantling of your tent and building your temple. And it looks a little like the first years of Solomon's reign.

There's a reason you haven't entered into your rest. There are those in your midst who came along from the old season and don't want to let the tent go. They vie for dominance. They liked things the old way. They cling to what was owed to them.

Before construction begins, expect a shake-up. No one expects it. You finally get to the place of giving God your "yes." You die to old visions, reboot, and are ready to build according to pattern.

And this is when the wolves come out to play. The shaking that happens between Tabernacle and Temple is a time of exposure. This is where you're most likely to experience betrayal.

The Jezebels in your midst will take a stand. The Adonijahs will denounce you. They will be the first in line to call you a false apostle. However, don't be discouraged. It was always going to be this way.

## Smoke Those Snakes Out!

It's part of the process. Before you can establish the Temple, the snakes must be smoked out.

Durban, South Africa is famous for its sugar cane fields. Those fields are also famous for housing black mambas, puff adders, and cobras. Because sugar cane is harvested by hand, before cutting, the fields are set on fire.

Old debris is burned up and as you guessed it... the snakes are smoked out. Harvesting can proceed.

When Craig and I faced this part of our process, we were blindsided by the snakes exposed by the fire. There were some who we imagined building with us for years into the future.

They were the first to betray us. They tried to topple our ministry. They went behind our backs to pull others to their side. (Welcome to the trenches of ministry! Our story isn't unique)

I began doubting my decisions.

"Lord if only we had stayed with our tent, this wouldn't have happened!"

"Lord if only we were wiser and didn't put our team in such a challenging environment, things would be different."

The Lord's response had me stumped. He said, "Colette, they were always going to betray you. So I let you into circumstances that would force their hand."

Whoa! God deliberately sent us on a journey to smoke out the snakes. He didn't want them to have any part in what was to come next.

Adonijah and Joab never saw the Temple. Judas never got to see the resurrected Christ. The snakes got smoked out before the glory fell.

So don't beat yourself up over it. Those that left you, were always going to leave. The nature of a snake was always in them. The fire you endured exposed the truth.

> THE NATURE OF A SNAKE WAS ALWAYS IN THEM. THE FIRE YOU ENDURED EXPOSED THE TRUTH.

Thank the Lord, they did it now! In fact, it's because they left that you can enter into your era of peace!

## MINDSET SHIFT REQUIRED

Before Solomon commenced construction, God's people needed to have the correct mindset. They had to get out of their war mindset and realize that they were in a time of peace. They had to come to rest and allow their creativity to come out of them so that they could build.

Up until then, they just knew war. They didn't build houses. They lived in houses that had already been built, remember? Solomon brought in an era of establishing through building, but the people needed to be ready for it.

People had to be positioned and circumstances had to be in line. A new culture needed to be established. The people needed to change their focus from war to building. In the same way that Solomon had to be positioned, God has been doing the same thing in the Church these past years.

## FIVEFOLD MINISTRY POSITIONING

He has positioned all of the fivefold ministers. He sent the prophets, to the darkest and most unholy churches where they deny the move of the Spirit.

He sent teachers to cultures and denominations bound in darkness.

It was so that we could prepare the hearts of God's people for the coming move. We needed to decree, release, pray, and intercede. God picked up His teachers, pastors, and evangelists, and He planted them in countries that they didn't expect. He planted them in social circles that they didn't imagine belonging to.

God has positioned His fivefold ministers for years. We started our first Prophetic School in 1999. For every single one of those years, I've seen God place His prophets in the craziest of places. They're sent to do one thing - to get on their face and declare the Word of God in the earth.

## The Fruit That Remains

Decades later, we stand on the fruit of those giants who gave up everything to declare the Word of God. God began this "new thing" a very long time ago. We just need to get the memo, find our part to play in it, and begin moving forward.

Stop and look back. You've been positioned many times. Every time God plucked you up, you thought, "Phew! I finally reached the end of that."

No, you didn't reach the end. It has always been an evolution. You were placed again and removed again, placed again and removed again. Do you know what? You weren't the only one!

Other apostles were sent to the wilderness. God placed some with sheep and goats. Some He placed in the middle of nowhere and took away their thriving ministry. He stripped them, challenged them, and sent them to Arabia.

Just when they thought that they were going to the Jews, He sent them to the Gentiles.

## Respecting the Pages of Your Story

Flip through the pages of your process. God was positioning and preparing you. He set you up for evolution all along. If you read all the prophetic words and the history of our Church in the last decade, can't you see the pages of your story?

You are so quick to tear the pages out of your book, but you don't recognize that they have made you who you are? God has positioned you time and again. All of those placements were another page in your book.

Tell me, what is your next chapter going to look like? That is what God is doing in His Church. I love this next part that I will call, construction.

## Gathering God's Generals

> **1 Kings 8:1** *Now Solomon assembled the elders of Israel and all the heads of the tribes, the chief fathers of the children of Israel, to King Solomon in Jerusalem, that they might bring up the ark of the covenant of the Lord from the City of David, which is Zion.*

Solomon built the Temple, but he didn't have the Ark in place yet. So, he had to assemble the elders.

Solomon could not complete the Temple alone, and in the same way, we cannot complete our mandates alone. You may understand what all needs to be taken care of for your mandate. Plot twist! You are not going to finish the mandate on your own.

Moses could not finish it alone. Joshua could not finish it alone. Solomon could not finish it alone. Paul could not finish it alone. Peter could not finish it alone.

## DNA Exchange

A spiritual DNA exchange is required. You need that missing piece for your mandate. Think about this for a second. Do you remember how long it took you to get the anointing, and to preach and minister the way you do? How much training did you go through, at the hand of the Holy Spirit, to be able to function in ministry the way that you do?

Depending on your call, it took time. Especially because you're an apostle, your training took years! For every call and mandate, you have to be shaped, changed, and trained. You don't have the time to go through this process that many times to get all the DNA that you need to complete your mandate!

Paul went through his process and Peter went through his. Being that they were both apostles, they could share in one another's wisdom, knowledge, and DNA. This way, each of them could finish their respective mandate.

They needed pieces from each other. Paul needed that piece of affirmation from James. Peter needed that piece from Paul, to fully understand what it meant to have a new covenant.

> **2 Peter 3:15** *and consider that the longsuffering of our Lord is salvation—as also our beloved brother Paul, according to the wisdom given to him, has written to you,*
> **16** *as also in all his epistles, speaking in them of these*

*things, in which are some things hard to understand, which untaught and unstable people twist to their own destruction, as they do also the rest of the Scriptures.*

Peter especially makes mention of Paul regarding his doctrine. Paul added the missing piece to Peter that God didn't give him. It's the same with us.

## Adding the Missing Pieces

So yes, it's high time that we see more prophets and apostles working together. It's long overdue for apostles to learn to work with other apostles. Why? It's because we need each other.

You don't have time, Apostle, to go through another 40 years of training for this missing strand of DNA that you can get from another apostle in five minutes flat. They have already gone through the journey and the death. They have the anointing and they have lived that entire process.

> YOU DON'T HAVE TIME, APOSTLE, TO GO THROUGH ANOTHER 40 YEARS OF TRAINING FOR THIS MISSING STRAND OF DNA THAT YOU CAN GET FROM ANOTHER APOSTLE IN FIVE MINUTES FLAT.

Yet, we are selfish people. We want the glory for ourselves. We want to be able to say, "I did it. Just me and Jesus. I climbed up that mountain all by myself."

Even Moses had Joshua to give him a little help up that mountain. Not even Moses climbed the mountain by himself. Correction. There was one time. It was the last time he climbed it and he never returned.

If you're going to complete your mandate, you need some missing pieces from others.

You don't have the full picture. Every one of the Twelve disciples had a piece to add to our New Testament Church foundation. How much more for today's Church era? You need that missing piece and God is going to open the doors for the Church to truly become universal.

We're seeing such an exchange of missionaries and that's just one function in the body of Christ.

Look around you. For those who are internationally connected, you know what I'm talking about. God is sending all of the fivefold ministry across nations.

We need what others in the universal Church have! There needs to be an exchange. If we are going to become a body, our parts need to become connected. The same blood needs to flow through our entire body. This means that we have to start finding something to connect on.

## Finding Connection

The Church has been too segregated for way too long. I'm not just talking about race here. Not to sound politically incorrect, but that's the least of our worries in the Church. Let's just talk about denomination, culture, language, and doctrine.

We're so divided on so many levels we cannot count them all. Yet, God has positioned apostles in unforeseen territories. I've connected with apostles called to take territory in the LGBTQ+ community. Another was sent of the Lord into boardrooms of millionaires to pattern regulations and edicts.

These apostles have a piece for me that I can enter into, and I have a piece to give them. They cannot fathom my process, but I can add a piece to them. When we share that DNA strand we are joints that connect one part of our arm to the other.

## Establishing a Kingdom

The Lord said to me, "I'm about to connect massive ministries together. They're not going to stand alone anymore. For a season, I established my megachurches, and everyone had their empires and big buildings, but evolution is coming.

I needed seasons past to shake my Church out of it's religious mindset. I needed a non-denominational thrust to shake them loose so that they could think in a way that they never thought in before.

However, now that the work is done, I desire to establish them each with a specific function. They must connect to become a kingdom."

We're about to see greater connectivity internationally than we ever have. We already see the signs. It's no longer about my church, or my community, or my country.

## Extending Your Reach

When God speaks about His Church, He holds the globe in His hand. You and I are both a part of that. Now we are talking about the gold, the finishing touches.

We will see preachers in one stream, having preached a certain doctrine, begin sounding like another stream. Is that compromise or an exchange of spiritual DNA?

*AS APOSTLES, WE GO THROUGH SO THAT OTHERS CAN ENTER INTO THE FRUIT OF OUR LABOR.*

Enter into someone else's labor. As apostles, we go through so that others can enter into the fruit of our labor.

As one apostle to another, we can receive the overflow from one another's labor.

Remember, our foundations remain diverse. Apostle Paul said that he would not build on another man's foundation. However, to get the roof set in place, networking is required. Without alignment with Hiram, Solomon couldn't complete the job.

## An Apostolic Network

I see an apostolic network in the Spirit. I see a connection of ministries at many different levels. Connections will form at larger levels with large ministries. Then, I see it happening with smaller ministries – these are runners with their feet on the ground.

These are like the synapses in our brains. You have a prophet there, an evangelist there, a pastor there. You have a home cell leader here. God will start connecting everyone, not so that they can come under one great apostle, but so that we can have joints to our body.

We need to be connected and have the same blood flowing through our veins. We need to stop poisoning each other. Can we rub off on one another without it becoming a power play? This is what God is establishing.

*CAN WE RUB OFF ON ONE ANOTHER WITHOUT IT BECOMING A POWER PLAY?*

Has God been opening doors for you, and has He been putting you through some pressure situations? Has He been digging out what you don't have and what you need?

You have been seeking God for a greater anointing. Could it be that you need the DNA that someone else has?

## Your Spiritual DNA Will Come Through

Keep in mind though, that just as the furnishings of the Tabernacle remained, so also will your spiritual DNA always shine through. In fact, I bet you can trace that one DNA strand that never left you. The way you minister today looks nothing like it did ten years ago. The way you dress today is not how you dressed 20 years ago.

However, there will always be an element of your spiritual DNA that will remain in each blueprint that finds its way into your hands. For Craig and me, that spiritual DNA has always been that of parenting and coaching. It's so intertwined in our DNA that no matter what pattern I get and what pattern Craig builds, you'll find this particular character of our DNA shining through!

Whether I'm leading someone to the Lord, starting a new business venture, or establishing a new ministry, that one DNA strand remains. I mentor unbelievers into salvation. I parent someone into a successful business. I just cannot run away from it. This is the nature of God that He formed in me. So yes, the blueprints will often take on different expressions, but your spiritual DNA will always shine through!

So how about it, Apostle? Is your temple well established? If so, then fantastic! Just two more realms to go and you're all set. Moving on to the next… your business realm. Yup, let's talk about money!

# 13

## THE BUSINESS REALM: YOUR SHIPS OF TARSHISH

*1 Kings 6:7 And the temple, when it was being built, was built with stone finished at the quarry, so that no hammer or chisel or any iron tool was heard in the temple while it was being built.*

An interesting fact about Solomon's Temple-building project is that he didn't mix it with business. Not even a hammer was heard in the Temple. Workers hammered in the quarries to cut stone. All the workers were a distance from the building site.

In other words, although they needed the gold for the Temple, they kept the dust of work at the quarry and the beauty of worship in the Temple! Here is a problem though. When you're fully established in your ministry, what was once uncomfortable has now become familiar. Your

> ALTHOUGH THEY NEEDED THE GOLD FOR THE TEMPLE, THEY KEPT THE DUST OF WORK AT THE QUARRY AND THE BEAUTY OF WORSHIP IN THE TEMPLE!

weaknesses are now your strengths and you cannot imagine seeing yourself doing anything else.

I get you! This is my story. The Lord took some time to shape me for my call and when I felt as if I was going to stay there forever, He began tapping me on the shoulder. He started to stretch me in the realm of business. The same insecurity I felt when I began the work of the ministry, reared its ugly head once again.

"Why can't I just do ministry?" However, the Lord kept tapping until I realized that until I invested in my business road, I was immature. I was imbalanced. So, once He had finally wrestled me to the ground, I made the classic mistake of trying to squeeze this business realm into my ministry.

You know… bring my insecurity into my place of familiarity. Yeah, that didn't work out very well. Before long I got the memo. Ministry was ministry and business was business. A massive shaking came to our ministry and along with it, the Lord gave Craig and me clear direction. We were to set up different teams. One team's focus could be ministry and another's could be administration and finances. I called my team, the B Team (Business Team) and together we carried the load.

We began to diversify and recognize that to ensure that money was never a driving force behind what we did, we had to make the lines clear. There's a lot of confusion regarding this pesky subject in the Church. I've seen more than one leader bringing business into the Church simply because they know how ministry works! It's their comfort zone.

So, they end up putting the money, business, and ministry together and bring the workers into the Temple. Next thing you know, they're walking around in their filthy shoes having come in from the quarry. They're scuffing up the beautiful floors of the Temple.

When you don't realize that you're meant to be establishing all three realms distinctly, you get confused and try to bring it together.

Solomon didn't bring it together. The Temple was the Temple, his palace was his palace, and his trade and business were his trade and business.

You need the anointing. That is why you have to establish the Temple first. You need your pattern, you need to know your calling, and you need to know where you're headed.

> MAKE NO MISTAKE, YOU NEED THE POWER OF GOD FOR ALL THREE REALMS.

Make no mistake, you need the power of God for all three realms. You need the anointing, a pattern, and a team for each road. That is why it's a smart idea to begin building the temple. Become established in your mandate, pattern, and anointing first.

Congratulations! You are a third of the way there. Good news is that while the rules change quite significantly when you work on your business realm, you get to bring the anointing right along with you!

Reality check: Without the Holy Spirit, the Spirit of Christ, dwelling within you, you may as well just be like the world. I can tell you to go and start a business and make lots of money. Anybody can do that in the world.

# Develop Your Business Pattern

> ***Colossians 3:1*** *If then you were raised with Christ, seek those things which are above, where Christ is, sitting at the right hand of God.*
> *2 Set your mind on things above, not on things on the earth.*

Having established your ministry first, you've learned to see things God's way. You have a heavenly perspective. Your mind has been renewed to ensure that you see everything through the eyes of the Word. This is going to be your anchor in the years ahead as you learn to walk the business streets.

I'm reminded of when Jesus washed the feet of His disciples and He said to Peter that not all of him needed washing because his body was already washed. His feet had become dusty though from walking in the world. (John 13:8-10)

If you take time in His presence, He makes your whole body clean! The time is coming when you'll indeed walk in the world for business and when you do, only your feet will need washing! Yes, the contamination will be there, but you'll easily identify it and not give way to it.

You need to have your mind shaped to think God's thoughts and feel God's heart. Then, you can step out into areas that touch the world, and you can bring Christ with you.

## Changing Business Mindsets

That is why, if you're on the opposite end of this story, and you've always been in business and not ministry, when you receive your calling, God is going to tell you to cut that off completely and put your all into ministry. I'm reminded of greats such as John G. Lake and Smith Wigglesworth who were both successful businessmen whom the Lord called to the work. First order of business? Give up all your business mindsets!

So, if you started with the business realm and then God calls on you to establish your ministry, expect a sudden shift. He will take away that strength and so He should, because your mind has been conformed to the things of the world.

Look, is it wrong to do it the world's way? This isn't merely logistics.

Yes, you can get rich applying practical principles taught in the world.

"I must be blessed because I got rich."

Yes, but then don't call yourself a minister because it's not about doing business and getting rich. It's about doing it God's way.

## You Are Not of This World!

When people see you wealthy in your business road, they should recognize that you're in this world, but you're not of it. They should recognize that you're a city on a hill, a lighthouse in the middle of the ocean.

You are successful, not because of your own grit and tenacity but because of someone else who's greater than you.

I know my own fair share of excellent businessmen. Some were mentored. Some were raised in entrepreneurial families. Some simply gritted their teeth and kept their dreams alive until they got their break. Nothing wrong with that. Jesus didn't condemn the rich young ruler! He never looked down His nose at the influential Centurion who called on Him. However, on the other hand, don't stand up and say, "God has made me the success I am today."

## WHO REALLY MADE YOU RICH?

No, you made yourself rich! Do you know who God is raising up in these end-times to become known as business or marketplace apostles? He is raising up those who didn't make it in the world, those who were failures and could not rub two cents together.

God is raising up His Josephs out of prison by a mighty move of His hand to put them on thrones. These apostles can truly say, "I stand by His grace alone."

Solomon didn't become wealthy because he had a few

good ideas. What did God give to him even before he started trade? He gave him wisdom.

He asked the Lord for wisdom and the Lord said, "Okay, I will give you wisdom, knowledge, and wealth." Solomon overflowed with ideas. Perhaps you've been struggling to get ideas. Have you been struggling with your finances?

Do you know why? It's because you're trying to fight with the wrong weapons. You are in the world, trying to do it the world's way, and fight the world's way. The enemy is a little more adept at this than you are. He has been doing it a lot longer.

## THE HOLY SPIRIT DIFFERENCE

> ***2 Chronicles 14:11*** *And Asa cried out to the LORD his God, and said, "LORD, it's nothing for You to help, whether with many or with those who have no power; help us, O LORD our God, for we rest on You, and in Your name we go against this multitude. O LORD, You are our God; don't let man prevail against You!"*
> ***12*** *So the LORD struck the Ethiopians before Asa and Judah, and the Ethiopians fled.*

You need to level the playing field and use something that the world doesn't have. You need the power of the Holy Spirit. His wisdom, and His anointing! This is the kind of power that Asa had at his back. You do the math in this encounter. Asa had an army of 300,000 men. The Ethiopians had 1,000,000 men. Things weren't looking good.

The rules of warfare stacked against Asa, so he pulled out an ace card the enemy didn't have... the power of God!

Now, just before you say that perhaps Asa was just a great strategist, keep on reading that passage. Not only did they win the war, but they had abundant plunder and went on further to defeat all the cities around Gerar.

> ***2 Chronicles 14:14*** *Then they defeated all the cities around Gerar, for the fear of the LORD came upon them; and they plundered all the cities, for there was exceedingly much spoil in them.*

They didn't just win, guys! Asa obliterated the enemy and came home a hero with more plunder than they could carry! Sure, worldly principles will work. You will win your war. However, will you experience circumstances that lend themselves to you in such a way that the dominoes keep falling?

You need more than a natural solution. You need some power in your corner.

## How You Develop That Power

> ***Deuteronomy 8:18*** *"And you shall remember the LORD your God, for it's He who gives you power to get wealth, that He may establish His covenant which He swore to your fathers, as it's this day.*

Don't overswing the pendulum on me here and think that you can just pray your financial battles through without putting in a day's work! Balance, people! Let's balance it out here.

You should know by now how the Holy Spirit trains you, Apostle. He trained your arms for war and you battled your ministry through to victory. The Lord led you to the right people and arranged the circumstances for you to excel. Developing your business realm is no different.

Training is involved. So, don't be surprised if the Lord stops telling you to pray and starts telling you to study to show yourself approved. Just because we should be receiving our wisdom from the Lord, doesn't mean you just sit on your couch waiting for a revelation. No, the revelation of the Lord always requires action.

> THE REVELATION OF THE LORD ALWAYS REQUIRES ACTION.

# 1. Study to Show Yourself Approved

The Word tells me that Solomon was a very well-studied man.

> *1 Kings 4:32* *He spoke three thousand proverbs, and his songs were one thousand and five.*
> *33 Also he spoke of trees, from the cedar tree of Lebanon even to the hyssop that springs out of the wall; he spoke also of animals, of birds, of creeping things, and of fish.*

This is not a King that just sat on his throne all day long. He used the wisdom God gave him. He applied it and studied the world around him. You want God to give you a fresh impartation of wisdom, but you're not using what you already have.

*WISDOM WALKS. WISDOM CRIES OUT. WISDOM BUILDS.*

Wisdom walks. Wisdom cries out. Wisdom builds. For when you walk out the wisdom you have, you receive the next step. The Lord will give you wisdom but if you never step out in it, you're never going to see where it will lead you.

This is how the Holy Spirit imparts His power to you to create wealth. It's not just an anointing for favor. Rather it's a power that positions you so that when God applies the power, doors open. Houses are built. Things happen!

Now, this is going to require effort on your part.

The power for wealth is received by sowing and reaping. You sow the wisdom you have and once it produces fruit, it will give you the next step to take. With every step of obedience you take, you receive a more of His power.

*WITH EVERY STEP OF OBEDIENCE YOU TAKE, YOU RECEIVE A BIT MORE OF HIS POWER.*

Do you understand now why the Lord led you in such a new direction? Perhaps He led you in a business realm that you have no clue about. Fantastic! He is poised to empower you! Come now, Apostle, how did you receive the anointing you flow in behind the pulpit?

## Embrace the Business Realm Process

Did someone just walk over to you one day and BAM you could preach? Hardly. You had to die to self. God required you to go through a process to shape you into a vessel that could carry His power.

The same process holds true for the business realm. Only the realm is different. The principles stay the same! This time you learn to have your arms strengthened!

The first step that the Holy Spirit will open to you to develop this business realm is study - to observe and to become educated. In 2 Chronicles 1:12 the Lord tells Solomon that he will grant him both wisdom and knowledge. Think about that. How does one impart knowledge to another?

Simply put, God leads you to knowledge! In other words, the Lord will open up ways for you to study. He will tell you where and what to learn. He will lead you to a coach or mentor. Although you might receive some of your studies from materials found in the world, it's the Holy Spirit who will lead you to that study.

> THE LORD WILL OPEN UP WAYS FOR YOU TO STUDY. HE WILL TELL YOU WHERE AND WHAT TO LEARN.

He will set your curriculum and as you stick to His study plan, you'll receive knowledge and along with it wisdom. As you put these two together and walk in obedience, you'll also stand in His power. It will be the kind of power that goes before you and arranges circumstances!

## 2. Positioning Through Obedience

When the Lord had Craig and me establish our own teams we began an evolution that put strength in place of our weakness. For me, this meant taking charge of the business team. Pray tell... what on earth does a girl from South Africa with just high school have to offer the world regarding business?

I got married right out of home. I never had to provide and before I could enter the marketplace, I was pregnant back-to-back with my first two daughters. Talk about unqualified! So, when God tapped me on my shoulder, trust me when I say, I shivered in my boots!

I kept trying to convince Him that Craig was surely the one to take charge of this business side of things! However, you know how the Father can be when He gets an idea in His head. He didn't let up. So here we go then, full steam ahead. Then at the beginning of 2019 we went through further shifts and changes.

Our ministry went through an upheaval and it was up to me and my team to find solutions! We had a shakeup in our ministry in South Africa. The apostolic leadership we had placed there decided to leave, leaving a school full of students that needed to be cared for. We got on our faces before the Lord.

I journaled, prayed and studied the Word every day with just one question, "Lord what are we going to do here?" He started to teach me. He led me to books, websites and people. Within a short time, a new structure came together. We integrated all of our divisions and moved everything online, using a system that was still quite unknown by the majority called Zoom.

We initiated class connects, set up a completely new system for our courses and lecturers. My team and I spent all of 2019 doing just one thing: Seeking God every single day for the next step He wanted us to take with our finances, administration and systems. We studied programming and as God led us, transitioned everything until it was flowing like clockwork.

March 2020 hit, and churches were shut down. Not only didn't we miss a beat, but our ministry soared. We were positioned. Everything we had implemented the two years prior came into its own and while many scrambled for solutions, we were up and running.

I only share our story with you because you don't realize how much God has positioned you. When you allow the Holy Spirit to train you, He will position you.

You see, when I talk about "power to create wealth" everyone imagines receiving the idea to end all ideas that will make them super rich. God's power does a lot more than that. When you do things His way, you don't need to fear for the future. You don't need to fear who wins the election or what is going to happen if a recession hits.

In fact, you can rest assured that no matter what is coming your way, God has already prepared and positioned you for it. Now, if all you go by is the world's news and their worldly wisdom, you'll get stuck. The world's doctrine declares that it all depends on you! Their principles aren't bad but following them is much like gambling. You could win. You could lose.

With the Holy Spirit at the table, you always win!

## 3. Send Out Your Ships

I'm thinking that Solomon was probably one of the first recorded arms dealers in the bible! He imported horses and chariots from Egypt and then sold them at a profit to the Hittites and kings of Syria. (1 Kings 10:29)

He traded by sending ships to Tarshish. He didn't keep his wisdom with him at home. Everyone has a good idea, but until you sow that idea, you'll remain poor!

*EVERYONE HAS A GOOD IDEA, BUT UNTIL YOU SOW THAT IDEA, YOU'LL REMAIN POOR!*

You keep speaking about what you're going to do "one day" when things "open up." When Solomon took the throne, his first order of business (after chopping a few heads) was to connect with Hiram to begin trade.

He didn't wait for the trade routes to find their way to him. Rather he initiated them! I'm pretty sure that a few ships got lost along the way. The ocean is unpredictable! Perhaps you've faced a few "lost ships" and you're too afraid to step out again. You are playing it safe now.

You might be safe, but are you at the place God has promised you yet? If ever you had excuses to keep safe, it's in the middle of a pandemic that has the world turning upside down. Don't you wish you had taken those risks earlier? However, you didn't and all you have is now in front of you.

The truth is that you're never going to find the perfect circumstances to step out in faith. You see... faith is just as active as wisdom is. It has to be applied. It means having the courage to step out and to fail. Then to get up and go again. How many more years do you want to keep wandering in the wilderness? Yes, you could live off donations for the rest of your life, but when your finances are dependent on how much people like you, you have a problem.

> *FAITH IS JUST AS ACTIVE AS WISDOM IS. IT HAS TO BE APPLIED. IT MEANS HAVING THE COURAGE TO STEP OUT AND TO FAIL.*

You can only be blessed as much as you keep the image people want to see. You will always remain confined to a ministry that depends on the kindness and generosity of others. Nothing wrong with it. Please don't misunderstand, I'm not knocking it. What I'm saying though is, when are we going to grow up? Can we enter maturity already?

## TAKING STEPS FORWARD

2019 feels like a lifetime away. Since then, the Lord has continued to position us. Only now, He uses us to equip others. We founded a new ministry called Apostle's Digest to give emerging prophetic and apostolic leaders a platform.

Where Craig and I had to fight for every book we published, we send our ships out now on behalf of others. The Lord leads us to men and women of God who are found in the trenches. Humble leaders who are up to their elbows in bringing healing and deliverance with principles they learned on their battlefields.

Poverty, sickness, and demons surrounding them, they have pushed through with a message that the Church needs to hear.

The catch being of course that no one wanted to listen. Who wanted to hear what a pastor of a little church in the poor side of town had to say? Well, God wants their voice heard and He uses the vehicle we built to get it out.

Never think that your process belongs to you. Once you've reached maturity in the business realm recognize that this is only the beginning. I will, however, stop right here on this subject and leave the rest for its own book.

Suffice it to say that until you get off your podium and allow the Lord to develop your business realm to the same level of maturity as your ministry realm, you'll always have an open door for satan to take you out. You will continue in immaturity and be continually hindered in your ministry.

## Each Realm Follows a Clear Pattern

Solomon's trading routes firmly established his kingdom. David took a very impressive collection for Solomon to build the Temple. However, you'll read that Solomon took all of this wealth and put it in the treasury once the Temple had been built. He didn't use it. He sent his own ships out!

When you look at doing business God's way, you realize that not only will you establish a foundation, but you'll cover it with gold. Solomon didn't just make any old temple.

You are crying out to the Lord and saying, "Lord, I want to reach the nations. Lord, I want to do more than just have church on Sunday."

Let's just face some realities. If you want to do those things, and accomplish that vision, it will take money. It will take wealth. If you haven't established this financial road of yours, you'll have a sad-looking temple.

They had the law of God in that Temple. They had the Ark of the Covenant in that Temple. You would think that would be good enough. Let's just put in the Ark and throw up any old curtain. However, Solomon didn't do that.

## Is Your Temple Going to Remain?

The Temple was magnificent. It was renowned through all the land. People came to just gaze upon it. They still speak about it generations later. So, tell me, what kind of temple do you want? Do you want it to remain?

It will take some financial aid and it doesn't mean only using the world's resources. Let me tell you something: Solomon was always at the top of the food chain. He was always the one calling the shots.

## Switching up Our Money Mentality

He knew which resources to get and the world did his work. Why? It was so that he could establish the Temple and make it look good. However, we are trying to suck the Church dry.

They have nothing left. Yes, the children of God should learn to give. When we give, we are blessed.

When we sow, God blesses us back. That is why we give. However, the doctrine on tithing is not going to buy us gold-covered planks.

Let's just put it where it's at. Where is the real money coming from in the Church? The business leaders! They feel guilty because they're not doing any real ministry and they just want to bribe God with money.

Being doubly honest, the pastor is only too happy to take that money because he doesn't have to go out and work. We have to take responsibility for all three realms. You will learn that you'll be stronger in one road than the other.

## What Does Your Business Realm Look Like?

What is your business pattern? What does your business realm look like right now? If you had a new believer come to your door saying, "I need to make money to feed my family."

Would you know what God's way of making money is?

"I will leave that for someone that's better qualified."

If you're a leader in the body of Christ, you better be qualified. If someone knocked on your door and said, "Teach me about the gifts of the spirit. Teach me how to raise my kids."

"No problem."

However, if someone says, "I have a financial problem."

"Oh, look at the time. Maybe we should schedule a meeting for another time. Here is a little donation."

## THE BUSINESS REALM: YOUR SHIPS OF TARSHISH

No, the Church needs more than donations. The financial support is fantastic, but what we need are trained leaders on the business road who have learned to tap into the power of God and the wisdom of Solomon, that can take those principles and get some gold into the Temple.

Then, the dross can be the silver and the bronze. When we reach this point, then we are starting to look like a Church that's a city on a hill.

Even these two realms, as beautiful as they were, it was no good without the palace.

First you establish your ministry realm and then the business. Once you've learned to establish these two realms, the Lord will say, "Great, the most important is for last. The social realm."

# 14

# THE SOCIAL REALM: BUILDING YOUR PALACE

*2 Chronicles 9:3 And when the queen of Sheba had seen the wisdom of Solomon, the house that he had built,*
*4 the food on his table, the seating of his servants, the service of his waiters and their apparel, his cupbearers and their apparel, and his entryway by which he went up to the house of the LORD, there was no more spirit in her.*

The social realm is the bridge between ministry and business. Where was the Queen of Sheba taken when she came to see the greatness of Solomon? She sure wasn't given a tour of the Holy of Holies.

No, she came to see him in his palace. Your social realm is the window to your life. If this realm is not a success, your ministry and business will fail. Solomon's palace was the showcase for his kingdom.

Without people, nothing is going to happen for you. Nobody has become a success sitting alone in their prayer closet. Yes, I'm not knocking the intercessors who are releasing the power of God. They should be doing that. They should decree.

However, until a preacher got out there on the missionary field, opened his mouth, and said something to people, nobody got saved. Until you learn to develop the social realm, I don't care how anointed you're, or how successful in business you're, you won't be fully equipped.

Your showcase has tinted windows, and no one can see the treasures hidden inside of you. If they cannot see what's inside, then they're not going to come closer to receive.

*YOU CAN BE FULL OF POWER, BUT UNTIL YOU REACH OUT AND PEOPLE CAN SEE AND RECEIVE THAT ANOINTING ISN'T GOING ANYWHERE.*

"If only people got to know me, they would see how anointed I am."

They won't get to know you if you keep yourself hidden. You can be full of power, but until you reach out and people can see and receive that anointing isn't going anywhere.

## RELATIONSHIPS ARE KEY

Tell me something... How good is business without relationships? How will you get a deal or make a sale?

If I don't like a salesperson, I don't buy from them. I sometimes look at them and think, "You just look funny and I don't like you." I don't care how good their product is. I just don't like them, and I won't buy their product because I don't trust them.

If you don't like somebody, you won't open your wallet and throw your money at them.

Dare you imagine that some people feel that way around you? Without relationships, your business will fail. Anybody successful in business, built relationships. Consider how much broken relationships have shattered you. Not just emotionally, but financially and spiritually. How many churches have dissolved because of splits and a breakdown of relationships?

*HOW MANY CHURCHES HAVE DISSOLVED BECAUSE OF SPLITS AND A BREAKDOWN OF RELATIONSHIPS?*

Remember when the Lord pulled you out of business or ministry to work on your marriage? Perhaps He pulled you aside to have children or to work with your ministry team. The Lord took Craig and me through a complete season of just making friends and connections. He pulled us out of the limelight to meet people and establish some good bonds that would be the strength of our ministry and business future.

## 1. Evolution of Your Identity

Perhaps you're here right now. The Lord just shut all the doors you were used to walking through to work on yourself. He has you working on your image, identity, and appearance.

I will never forget when the Lord told Craig and me to start working out on a regular basis. Now I had asthma as a child and doing anything physical brought back terrible memories. I was skinny and weak. Add to that, I was raised in a ministry family that looked down on sporty types. So... here we go again! Learning a completely new life skill!

Your palace encompasses the natural side of your life. Relationships, image, identity as a man or woman. It's your showcase. Turns out that the Lord needed Craig and me to have an image that matched our mandate.

I'm not going to lie, for the longest time I thought we were being so fleshly.

I was thinking, "Lord, what on earth does this have to do with ministry?"

Turns out, more than I realized! We needed to become physically fit for what God needed us to do.

How strange to tell people, "God told me to work out." Only to have our lives turned around with a pandemic! Long before COVID infections were at their peak, we had lost weight, had a workout routine and a healthy menu. Once again, we found ourselves positioned ahead of the times.

Don't underestimate the power you gain from allowing the Lord to work on your spirit, soul, and body! I know apostles whom the Lord is raising up who have a mandate in this area. Who would have imagined 20 years ago that we would see apostles in health and fitness?

So, allow me to give you a bit of heads up here. When the Lord begins calling on you to build your palace a couple of things are going to happen.

# WAKE UP TO THE SIGNS!

The first warning might be a sudden bout of sickness! High blood pressure, diabetes, overweight, or arthritis. I'm not advocating the doctrine that God delights in making us sick. Rather, I'm saying... don't you think it's time to wake up to the signs?

Your poor body cannot take much more! I consider how many great revivalists died before their time, because they didn't take care of themselves. If you refuse to listen, then the Lord is going to send people your way to begin getting your attention.

Craig and I held a workshop and he was leading worship. It was powerful and life changing. He was a bit out of breath and after the meeting an elderly gentleman walked up to him. He put his hand on Craig's shoulder and said, "Son, I noticed that you were quite out of breath after the worship. I just want to suggest that you look at losing some weight."

The gentleman didn't say it to be cruel, but was sharing a word from God. His message didn't go unnoticed! However, how often do you want to get offended at people who keep poking at your insecurity with your self-image? Could it be that the Lord is just trying to get your attention? Your doctor says you need to lose weight. Your chiropractor suggests a healthier lifestyle. Then, because it's not "spiritual" you think that you can just ignore the warnings.

Come aside with me here for a moment. In today's day and age with sickness rampant and a massive shift towards health and fitness, do you have any idea of the kind of image you portray if you don't build your palace? Solomon went to great lengths to make his palace look good and so should you! What is the first thing that people see when they meet you?

You see, the Queen of Sheba could not get a tour of the Temple. If Solomon didn't have his palace, where would he have hosted her? Do you really think she would have been impressed had she been entertained in a tent out back?

I hate that people judge on appearance. I hate that we are in a world where first impressions count. However, love it or hate it, here we are. What are you going to do about it, Apostle? It's time to stop blaming your circumstances, upbringing, and generational curses and to apply the wisdom that God has given to you!

## 2. Gain Favor by Keeping Up!

> ***Proverbs 3:4*** *And so find favor and high esteem in the sight of God and man.*

It was said of both Jesus and John the Baptist, that they gained favor with God and man. Wherever Jesus went, He gained favor in the world and amongst His own. I love this passage in Proverbs. It says to find favor and high esteem.

*FAVOR IS NOT GOING TO FIND YOU! YOU MUST SEEK IT OUT!*

In other words, favor is not going to find you! You must seek it out. The word "esteem" can also be translated as "understanding." In other words, you need to find ways that give you favor and allow people to see you! What is the point of having a great business or ministry and no one knows that you exist?

## THE SOCIAL REALM: BUILDING YOUR PALACE

Do you really think that just because you have a ministry that you're automatically known?

I remember God challenging me on this. I grew up a pastor's kid. I knew the Church. I was comfortable in the Church. I was always in ministry. I was the drummer in the band at 11. That was all I knew.

Then suddenly, the Lord thrust me into the world of business and money. He had me learning natural stuff like programming, designing book covers, formatting, and getting my grammar straight.

I said, "Lord, what does all this have to do with ministry?"

Just go and have a look at our bookshop and you'll see exactly how much it had to do with ministry. Had I not learned those natural things you would not be reading this book today.

Sure, we could've just hired somebody else. However, I love Apostle Paul who could say, "I don't build on another man's foundation." (Romans 15:20)

If there was a book to be written, I wrote it. If there was a cover to be designed, I designed it. I learned enough to impart that knowledge and anointing to my daughter, Jessica, who then became our graphics designer. She now uses her skills to design for other authors as part of her ministry. So, were all those natural strengths a waste of time?

This follows on so beautifully from what I shared concerning business. You keep praying that the Lord will send you someone who can put your name in lights, not realizing that you're called to be the source for others. You are an apostle! It's for you to find favor! It's for you to build your palace. Solomon spent seven years building the Temple and 13 years building his palace. So, don't be discouraged if the Lord keeps shutting doors on "the easy way out." He is maturing you and calling you to build!

## Social Media

I remember when the Lord told us to begin showcasing our ministry on social media years ago. I was dead against it. In my opinion, social media was the epitome of the flesh! However, the Lord pressed us, and we dipped our toes in the water. Little did we know that in remote countries such as South Africa, social media was their only exposure to the rest of the world. With rampant poverty, many can only access social media such as Facebook. Reason being that most phone carriers provide unlimited free access to such apps as Facebook and WhatsApp.

We began reaching an entirely new realm of believers by getting some savvy. Allow yourself to be stretched, Apostle!

Where does the Lord keep leading you? What platform does He keep putting in your face? Are you pushing against Him because of your man-made moral code or are you following in obedience to His instruction? If ever the Church was in the midst of an evolution, it's now.

If you're to be part of this movement then it's going to mean trying things you never have. It means learning new skills and having the courage to remain in uncomfortable environments.

## 3. Make Friends

Without relationships, your ministry and business are dead in the water.

## THE SOCIAL REALM: BUILDING YOUR PALACE

Your palace is the showcase for the rest of your life.

It was in the palace that Solomon judged between the two prostitutes. It was there in his throne room that he said, "Cut the child in two." Everybody was in awe of his wisdom. (1 Kings 3:16-28)

He wasn't having a praise party or sacrificing goats and sheep. He did that in the Temple. In his palace, he was a judge, leader, and king. He was showing the world, through natural means, what it looked like to be fully equipped - to be complete.

He showed the world what it looked like to have wisdom in spiritual things, business things, and natural things. If you cannot take the anointing from God and use it in these other areas, then you're not complete.

I would dare say that the social realm is the most neglected of all three in the lives of ministers.

Apostle, can you just be normal? Do you know how to sit down and have fellowship with somebody?

Can you drink coffee and have a relaxed conversation? Can you connect with tax collectors and prostitutes as Jesus did?

Not every conversation you have with an unbeliever is going to lead them to salvation! I'm not knocking evangelism, but sometimes can we just have a cup of coffee together?

*I'M NOT KNOCKING EVANGELISM, BUT SOMETIMES CAN WE JUST HAVE A CUP OF COFFEE TOGETHER?*

I don't judge because the Lord knows how badly I messed this up. Fortunately, the Lord allowed me to get away with it for a while because I have a husband who finds this easy. He can connect with anyone and I just left him to it.

I could not keep coasting on his grace though. I had to, as an apostle, discover my own. I didn't realize how far the Lord had brought me until Craig and I were visiting with some leaders. We had just finished a week-long workshop and before flying home, they were taking us around to see some sights in the region.

As we were standing in line waiting to enter a restaurant the lady behind us noticed Craig's rugby shirt and struck up a conversation with him. She was as worldly as they come. Foul language and part of the "party till you puke" set. We engaged her in conversation, learned her story and she learned that we were pastors. She opened right up!

The look on our host's faces, though! Okay, perhaps I shouldn't laugh so loudly while reading this, but... I cannot deal. They were horrified! As if every bad word burned their ears and this woman's wild ways offended their sanctification. They could not wait for the line to clear, to shoot ahead to the table waiting for us.

How crazy is it that the only time you can reach the lost is when they're brought to your church? What is wrong with us apostles, if we cannot have a conversation about sports, or our favorite movie?

We might not be of this world, but we are certainly in it, and perhaps a good dose of humility is required here. There is only one reason that you're highly favored, and that reason is because you have the indwelling of the Holy Spirit.

# THE SOCIAL REALM: BUILDING YOUR PALACE

***Philippians 2:3*** *Let nothing be done through selfish ambition or conceit, but in lowliness of mind let each esteem others better than himself.*
*4 Let each of you look out not only for his own interests, but also for the interests of others.*

Take Him away and you're nothing. You are not a better person than anyone else in the world. I think Paul says it pretty straight in the passage above. We have way too much spiritual pride. I'm elevated because of who He is and not because of who I am. I've seen so many leaders hide behind their spirituality as an excuse to look down their noses at those who don't share their station.

> I'M ELEVATED BECAUSE OF WHO HE IS AND NOT BECAUSE OF WHO I AM.

I'm reminded of the Pharisees who looked down on tax collectors. They forgot that they didn't choose the Lord, He chose them. They had nothing to boast of. I've met unbelievers who showed more kindness than believers. So, let's come down a few notches and make this treasure we have in our earthen vessels available to others.

I think that this is probably the greatest challenge I faced. I didn't realize just how much I hid behind my spiritual mask to hide my natural insecurities. When the Lord calls on you to build your palace, you also might not realize just how lacking you are in this area! It's only when you try to build the palace that you discover that if it wasn't for Christ, you would not have anything to go on!

So, lean on the strength you gained as you built your temple. However, realize that to open doors, you'll need to reach people who cannot have access to that Temple! Just as the Queen of

Sheba wasn't able to access the Temple, so others you reach will be sent of the Lord to open doors, but they'll do so through the palace!

## You Are the Pattern

> **Philippians 3:17** *Brethren, join in following my example, and note those who so walk, as you've us for a pattern.*

It's only when you've matured in all of these realms that you have the power to bring maturity to the Church. Only then can you do a whole lot more than get a pattern. Apostle, you become the pattern!

It's time to bust out of your limitation! Perhaps it has felt as if I've been putting you down, but step back for a moment and choose instead to embrace the challenge. I told one of my spiritual sons never to fear his mistakes. I said to him, "My mistakes inspire me! My failures are my inspiration to rise up!"

When I realize that I've failed, it's a training opportunity to become more than I'm in the moment. How hard it is for us to sometimes face the reality of our shortcomings? However, when you embrace your weaknesses and learn to "rejoice in your infirmities" you have the opportunity to grab the Holy Spirit's hand and to bring power into places of weakness.

> *WHEN I REALIZE THAT I'VE FAILED, IT'S A TRAINING OPPORTUNITY TO BECOME MORE THAN I'M IN THE MOMENT.*

I spoke to you about the power to create wealth. I spoke on the power the Holy Spirit has to impart in all three of these realms. How is this power received? It's received by recognizing and embracing our weakness. Only then do we qualify to hold onto His power. Is this such a great price to pay, Apostle?

You want to see the Church on fire for Christ. You want to see the poor fed and the downtrodden picked up. You want to see unity and fellowship in the Church. Well, to bring that kind of maturity to pass, you're going to need a whole lot of power. So, I think it's a pretty good idea to get some of that power in your life first before you can impart it to others.

Where is the Lord challenging you? Is He thrusting you into a new level of ministry? Have you covered your temple in gold? What about your trading ships? Have you established your trade routes? How is the construction of your palace coming along? Is your life the showcase that others can pattern their lives after?

I'm sure that as I've shared, I've pricked you on one or more of these points. Good. Now, what are you going to do about it? What use is it to get challenged, put the book down and then tell everyone what a conviction you got? When will your conviction become an action?

# Take Action

There comes a time when you just have to try and fail and then try again. Don't you realize that this is what shapes you? What do you have to lose today? The Lord is well able to give you another ministry. Another business opportunity is just another open door away.

Rather run headlong into failure than be caught saying, "I died never having tried." The Lord has gone to a lot of effort to bring you to the place you stand today. Your training and the price you've paid has purpose. Now finish the race, receive the power, and solidify the pattern to impart to others.

# About the Author

Apostle Colette Toach is a globally recognized apostolic leader, author, and spiritual mother whose life's work is dedicated to equipping believers to step fully into their God-given mandate. With Apostolic Evolution, she releases her 44th published book - continuing a legacy of clarity, depth, and transformational teaching for those navigating apostolic calling and spiritual process.

Together with her husband, Apostle Craig Toach, Colette co-founded Toach Ministries International, a global ministry focused on raising prophetic champions, building five-fold ministry teams, and helping leaders mature into their Kingdom assignments. Through books, online schools, mentorship programs, podcasts, and international training, her voice has shaped leaders across nations and generations.

Known for bridging spiritual revelation with practical application, Colette teaches with precision, authority, and compassion - addressing topics such as apostolic identity, spiritual cycles, leadership development, dreams and visions, and the inner transformation required to sustain long-term calling. Her message is rooted in abiding in Christ while courageously advancing the work of the Kingdom.

As a mentor and coach, Colette leads apostolic and author development programs that help believers bring their message to the world, establish healthy foundations, and build with wisdom and accountability. Her writing carries the voice of a guide who has walked the journey - inviting readers not just to grow, but to evolve.

Apostolic Evolution is an invitation to recognize where you are in your spiritual cycle and to embrace the transformation required for what God is doing next.

## Let's Build a Relationship

Find out more about me:
www.toach-ministries.com

Connect with me on Facebook:
www.facebook.com/ColetteToach

Follow me on Twitter:
https://twitter.com/ColetteToach

Find my books on Amazon:
www.amazon.com/author/colettetoach

Join our free Online Community:
http://www.apostolic-network.com

*About the Author*

Listen to our Apostles Digest Podcast on
**Spotify:** [Spotify Link](#)

# RECOMMENDATIONS BY THE AUTHOR

## The Apostolic Handbook

The Apostolic Handbook is the most detailed resource on the decisions you need to make in your apostolic call. I don't believe you'll find a guide more dedicated to making your journey clear and actionable.

Apostle Colette Toach is one of the church's experts in fivefold ministry leadership. She is known for simplifying the too-often mystified ministry roles into easy-to-follow guides. Here, she builds your knowledge of necessary functions in the apostolic. This includes mentorship, spiritual parenting, apostolic vision, and leadership. Illuminate your dark path with this enlightened teaching.

The Apostolic Handbook will reshape how you view your obedience to God and train you to think in a way that expands the kingdom of heaven daily. Achieve success that lasts and honor your Heavenly Father with a life that produces enduring results. Lead God's people with confidence and clarity.

You find *The Apostolic Handbook* on amazon.com. (https://a.co/d/6odxAhJ)

# Apostolic Mandate

**Your Apostolic Mission Explained in Detail**

Get all the information you could need about your unique apostolic mandate. Learn the detailed steps to working with a fivefold ministry team, driving God's vision forward, and leaving a lasting work for the body of Christ. This is a straightforward teaching about apostolic leadership that meets your unique spiritual DNA.

This book is designed to reveal your God-given anointing, authority, skill sets, and spiritual gifts in every chapter. It's not just for your knowledge but for practical application and impartation to your ministry team. This is everything you need to know to mature the church. You will learn:

- What your apostolic mandate is and the process God takes you through to form it. You'll also discover what God expects of you and how He empowers you to do it.

- How to create a fivefold ministry team to do a greater work than you can do alone. Discover the power of spiritual parenting and biblical mentorship.

- Steps to establishing your mandate in the earth to have a great impact on the church globally.

- Examples of apostolic mandates in the Old and New Testament: What we can learn from their failures and successes.

Apostle Colette Toach writes this book after decades of training apostles to grow their ministries and teams. What you discover is the path all apostles take to walk out their call with purpose. Apostolic leaders, apostles, prophets, teachers, and pastors have used this book to recognize the shift God has brought to their lives.

You find **Apostolic Mandate** on amazon.com. (https://a.co/d/aLLloOq)

www.ingramcontent.com/pod-product-compliance
Lightning Source LLC
Chambersburg PA
CBHW070059080526
44586CB00013B/1122